Jyotisha for Noobs

Sourabh Roy

नियत से नियति, नियति से भाग्य,
भाग्य से धर्म, धर्म के अनुसार कर्म,
कर्म से पुनर्जन्म ।

Intention decides destiny, destiny decides fortune, fortune decides dharma, dharma decides karma, karma decides re-birth.

Contents

Chapter 1	1
Planets	1
Symbols	4
Panchbhuta	5
Gender	6
Chapter 2	7
Creating a natal chart	7
Movable, Fixed, and Dual sign	9
Mooltrikona, Exaltation, Debilitation	9
Kaal Purush Kundali	11
Directions in a natal chart	16
Significance of twelve houses	16
Body limbs and different houses	17
Chapter 3	19
Planetary motion	19
Planetary aspects	20
Chapter 4	26
Moon's position and respective desires	26
Planets and colours	28
Chapter 5	30

Understanding Lagna and overall body   30

Planetary taste   34

Potential of a house in lagna(D1) Chart   36

Chapter 6   39

Zodiac span and degrees   39

Divisional charts   39

Computing D2 or Hora Chart   40

Computing D9 or Navamsa chart   44

Computing D60 or Shastiamsa chart   48

Chapter 7   58

Lordship of Shastiamsa   58

Chapter 8   69

Consciousness of a child   69

Chapter 9   71

Yogas in birth chart   71

Gajakesari yoga   73

Natural relationship   73

Temporary relationship   75

Compound relationship   75

Vipareet rajyoga   77

Amala yoga   78

Dharmakarmadhipati yoga   78

Solar yogas 79

Lunar yogas 80

Chapter 10 82

Planetary period or dasha 82

Nakshatras 82

Summary of using Vimshottari dasha 88

Chapter 11 89

Mundane astrology 89

Life path/Dharma 91

Career 93

Example chart 1 96

Example chart 2 100

Example chart 3 105

Key points 110

Chapter 12 113

Artha/Wealth 113

Chapter 13 116

Kama/Desire 116

Marriage or relationship 116

Sexual compatibility 118

Chapter 14 121

Moksha/Liberation   121

Past life in a chart   122

Miscellaneous   123

Vastu/Architecture   123

Initiation of mundane task   124

Do's and Don'ts   126

Preface

The idea that sprung forth what if someone cannot compile or read the entire Brihat Parasara Hora Shastra. Is there anyway to help such a person understand Jyotisha in lucid and step-wise instructions? A handout for do-it-yourself, and there is no other tool available to mankind than Jyotisha, which helps one understand oneself, about one's past, one's current fortunes or misfortunes. And to survive the vicissitudes of life when it seems knocking. Usually everybody becomes frantic when certain events happen in their life out of the blue and they can't find out the explanation why it is happening over and over again. People look for answers everywhere, whether from peers or astrologers. However, just like in any trade, there are a few bad apples which destroy the taste of the person eating them. Therefore, to fool someone in Jyotisha becomes very easy because the person is already frantic or hopeless. Jyotisha or any esoteric arts for that matter are intuitive, but intuition can be wrong, particularly when masked with ego, whereas a proper method or procedure which are reproducible removes the scope for such error. How many times you have met an astrologer or a palmist and realised the predictions are all generalised and don't contribute much to your needs? One size fits all never works, therefore it has to be tailormade for each individual. At the same time, it is a daunting task for an individual to compute all the possibilities concerning a person. This book will help any newbie or someone who has never been accustomed to the knowledge of Jyotisha, even people who don't want to do deep research. It is rather a succinct handout for people trying to find meaning in their natal chart. An astrological chart is a blueprint of the native-born on a specific day, on a specific time and location. No two people have the same fate. The change in seconds can change the inherent nature of a person at the core. Jyotisha means "Jyoti" and "isha", which means light of the divine.

Chapter 1

Planets

An astrological chart maps all the known planets: Sun, Moon, Mars, Mercury, Jupiter, Venus, Saturn, Rahu, also known as North Node, Ketu, also known as South Node. Consider a town that is owned by seven planets, and each of them is given the responsibility to cater to or train the person in this town. In this town, we have a man called Zaddy. Now we will witness how Zaddy finds his way through his astrological chart and glimpse of his karma. As we progress with Zaddy's life, readers can apply the same methods in their respective natal charts as well.

Sun is the head of the town. He is always bright, with valour and royalty. He is ready to sacrifice himself for the greater good of the town. His favourite colour is copper or orange. Moon is the round-faced queen and royalty, your favourite auntie that looks after everyone whether they have a roof over their head and food in their belly. She is emotional and fickle-minded. Her favourite colour is white. Mars is the physical tutor, an ex-army with an athletic build. A warrior who is always there to protect the town from outside threats. His favourite colour is blood red. Mercury is the young chap in the town who always cracks jokes even in the worst places. He is younger in his looks. He is hilarious, quirky, and intelligent. He doesn't have much physical strength. His favourite colour is green. Jupiter is the teacher in the town who sets the rules and guidelines for the sustainability of the entire town. He is tawny and has a belly. He doesn't like to quarrel and mind his own business. Yellow is his favourite colour. Venus is the beautiful woman for whom the whole town goes crazy. She likes the attention, she gets it everywhere she goes. She is charismatic, a damsel. Silver or variegated luxury is her favourite colour. Saturn is the oldest man in the town. He is a record keeper and a taskmaster. He compiles how much task has been completed and how much has not been. He is slow. He only understands black and white and nothing else. If something is in grey he will wait till it becomes black and white. He is impartial to every person in the town as well. Dark blue is his favourite colour.

Now, there are two outcasts in the town as well. Rahu is a mystical person sometimes good, other times bad, or even ugly. He is what he is, a shapeshifter. He can take the persona of all five planets but not Sun and Moon. Rahu holds a special enmity with the Sun because he can't shape-shift into the Sun. He doesn't have a body only a head. So whenever he tries to get close to the Sun the light from Sun reveals that he is a shapeshifter and not original because there is no shadow of him on the ground. Rahu's favourite colour is smoky, variegated. He is very cunning and his favourite is Mercury, the young chap whom he can control. Rahu is also comfortable with Moon, only for the moment she is proud. It is because the Moon requires a mirror and reflection, and Rahu shape-shifts into a mirror.

Ketu is also a mystical person but he loves isolation. He doesn't like to be bothered. He carries a scythe and can't see. He has intuitive powers and even without sight he knows the place very well where he sits. Ketu likes Jupiter because Jupiter doesn't bother him. So Ketu follows the sight of Jupiter only when he is with him. Due to a big scythe of Ketu whichever house he visits, he scraps off the paint of the walls or, dent and damage nook and corners. He can't help himself. Ketu's favourite colour is brown.

Only Mercury grows and gets better with time and so does the houses he sits or owns. And Saturn is old and slow, therefore the results come at a tortoise pace. Hence, wherever Saturn sits or owns also gets improved with time. For all other planets delivery of results remains the same throughout life.

Each planet has an animal associated with it which reflects its most inherent nature. Jupiter is represented by an elephant. Saturn is represented by a tortoise. Rahu is represented by dogs. Ketu is represented by cats. Mercury is represented by monkeys. Moon is represented by cows. Sun is represented by bulls. Mars is represented by a lion. Venus is represented by a parrot. Different animals and birds have a connection with deities not to be confused with planets. For example, the crow is a representation of ancestors of one's lineage or 'Pitrus' therefore connected with the deity Yama and not Saturn. Similarly, Swan is connected with Brahma, not to be confused with Jupiter.

Symbols

Each planet has its own short hands or symbols to identify as below:

Sun - ☉
Moon - ☾

Sourabh Roy

Mars - ♂

Mercury - ☿

Jupiter - ♃

Venus - ♀

Saturn - ♄

Rahu - ☊

Ketu - ☋

Panchbhuta

Each planet has associated characteristics in "panchbhuta" Or five elements other than the luminaries and nodes as below:

Sun- soul

Moon- desire

Mars- fire

Mercury -earth

Jupiter -ether

Venus- water

Saturn- air

Rahu- Illusion

Ketu- Introspection

Gender

The genders of the planets are as below:

Sun, Mars and Jupiter are Masculine.

Moon, Venus are Feminine.

Saturn - Neuter.

Mercury - Androgynous.

Chapter 2

Creating a natal chart

Now, let us create an astrological natal chart(north Indian style) in the below steps:

1. Draw a square
2. Connect the opposite vertices with a straight line.
3. Mark the mid-point on each side of the square.
4. From one mid-point, connect the other two adjacent mid-point using a straight line. It will form another square inside.
5. All twelve portions are mapped in Roman numbers from I- XII in anti-clockwise. These indicate houses or "bhavas".

Now, we will label each house with a sign (1-12). These signs correspond to different zodiac signs, Aries, Taurus, Gemini, Cancer, Leo, Sagittarius, Capricorn, Aquarius and Pisces, respectively. Wherever Roman numerals are used, it is house, and when natural numbers are used, it is the respective zodiac sign. It is not a thumb rule but for ease of

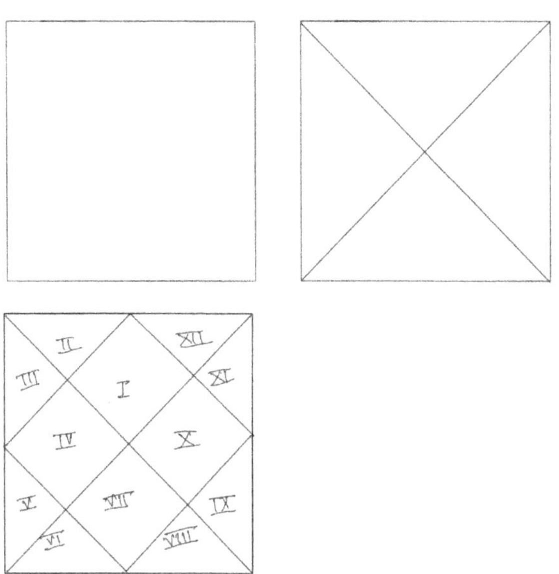

understanding, we will follow this system throughout this book.

Sun owns the zodiac sign of Leo(5).

Moon has lordship over Cancer(4), Mars over Aries(1) and Scorpio(8), Mercury over Gemini(3) and Virgo(6), Jupiter over Sagittarius(9) and Pisces (12), Venus over Taurus(2) and Libra(7), Saturn over Capricorn (10) and Aquarius (11).

The two nodes, Rahu and Ketu, don't own any house. However, they are significators of Aquarius (11) and Scorpio(8) respectively.

The signs are also classified into three categories, namely: **Movable, Fixed, and Dual sign**

Aries, Cancer, Libra, and Capricorn are movable signs.
Taurus, Leo, Scorpio, and Aquarius are fixed signs.
Gemini, Sagittarius, Virgo, and Pisces are dual signs.

Mooltrikona, Exaltation, Debilitation

Mooltrikona, exalted ("uchh") and debilitated ("neech") sign or "rashi" for each planet.

A mooltrikona rashi for a planet is his natural abode, which is like his home office. And an exalted rashi for a planet is like his leisure place. And debilitated rashi is a place where the planet doesn't want to be because it is forced against its primal nature, similar to your toxic boss, whose face spoils your entire day when you go to work.

Planet	Exaltation	Debilitation	Mooltrikona
Sun	Aries	Libra	Leo
Moon	Taurus	Scorpio	Cancer
Mars	Capricorn	Cancer	Aries
Mercury	Virgo	Pisces	Virgo
Jupiter	Cancer	Capricorn	Sagittarius
Venus	Pisces	Virgo	Libra
Saturn	Libra	Aries	Aqaurius
Rahu	Gemini	Sagittarius	Taurus
Ketu	Sagittarius	Gemini	Scorpio

Exaltation, debilitation, and mooltrikona all happen for the planet at certain degrees only. So even if a planet is present in a sign, the truest sense of exaltation, debilitation or mooltrikona happens in those span of degrees. The underlying reason for the above table is based on nakshatras, which is beyond the scope of this book. For the nodes, there are different opinions of exaltation and debilitation. But for your understanding, consider this. Rahu is the smoky shapeshifter. He can best control a kid or young curious chap. Gemini is such a sign that frolics and is young, therefore Rahu gets power and exaltation in Gemini as it is easy to manipulate a kid with candy however, he gets debilitated when he tries the manipulation in the sign of Sagittarius which is ruled by Jupiter. Jupiter catches his art of snake oil salesman. Rahu's mooltrikona becomes Taurus because the Moon is exalted in Taurus, and the Moon is in her leisure place. So again, the cowboy Rahu becomes a mirror and deceives the Moon that she is the most beautiful and no one else comes close. Whereas Ketu doesn't have a head, but he got a scythe and intuitive skills. So when he is in the sign of Jupiter, he automatically gets the best guidance and does not strike his scythe, avoiding damage. Hence, it gets exalted in Sagittarius and debilitated in Gemini. Exaltation, debilitation, and mooltrikona happen in zodiac signs or Rashi. It is not a concept for houses or bhavas.

Kaal Purush Kundali

The below chart is of Aries ascendant, also called the "Kaal Purush kundali" aka "Cosmic man astrological chart". "Kaala" means time, "Purush" means male, "Kundali" means astrological chart. This chart is used in Brihat Parasara Hora Shastra and the entire manuscript is explained keeping it as a reference. Therefore all those people whose ascendant or rising sign or first house happens to be Aries can directly apply the dictum mentioned in the afore-

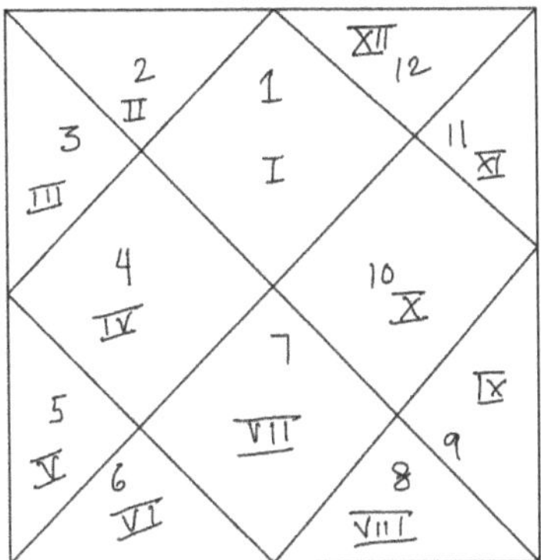

said book. Here we are going to look at a few different charts in the progressive chapters.

The twelve houses are classified as below:

First house- it is called the ascendant or rising or Lagna. And the planet owning that house is called ascendant lord or lagna lord. Here Mars is lagna lord.
Seventh house - it is called the descendant.

Note: When someone is born, the zodiac sign rising in the sky in the east direction becomes his ascendant. The calculations are based on observation of planetary movements. One can either refer to a Pachang for such planetary calculations and then map it on the natal chart. But with so much software available at our fingertips we don't need to compute that manually. Any software such as JHora, or drikpachang can do the job for you. Key in your birth details(date of birth dd-mon-yyyy, place(latitude and longitude), and time in 24-hr format) and it will create the chart for you.

There are four "upchaya" or progressive houses III, VI, X, XI.

These houses get better with time, therefore in cosmic man's chart these houses refer to the sign of Gemini, Virgo, Capricorn and Aquarius. The reason these signs improve with time is because Gemini and Virgo are ruled by Mercury which is a young chap, matures slowly with time. And Capricorn and Aquarius are ruled by Saturn which is slow as a tortoise. It ultimately reaches there but very slowly.

There are three trines or "kona" I, V, IX, so for cosmic man's chart these houses will be the sign of Aries, Leo and Sagittarius. It is also called trikona or trine of life.

There are four quadrants or "kendra" I,IV,VII, and X, so the corresponding signs in the above chart will be Aries, Cancer, Libra and Capricorn.

There are three evil or "trik" houses VI,VIII and XII, so the corresponding signs will be Virgo, Scorpio, and Pisces.

Now, let us take the chart of Zaddy, we will help him to figure out his path using our astrological skills.

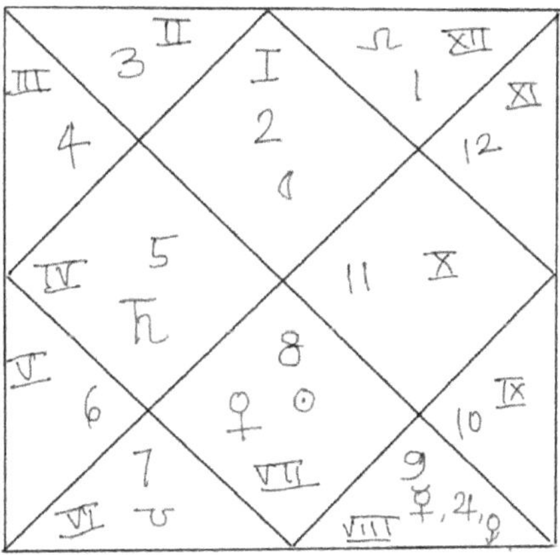

D1 chart

His ascendant sign becomes Taurus(2), descendant becomes Scorpio(8). The ascendant lord or lagna lord becomes Venus. Upchaya houses become the signs 4,7,11 & 12 in his chart. Trikona houses become the signs 2,6 and 10. Trik houses become the signs 7(Libra), 9(Sagittarius) and 1(Aries). Quadrant or kendra houses becomes the sign 2,5,8 and 11.

In the above natal chart, the Moon is placed in Taurus(2) in I house. Venus and Sun are placed in Scorpio(8) in VII house. Saturn is placed in Leo(5) in IV house. Mercury, Jupiter and Mars is present in Sagittarius(9) in the VIII house. Rahu is placed in Aries(1) in XII house and Ketu is placed in Libra(7) in VI house.

So planets in kendra houses are Moon, Saturn, Venus and Sun. Planets in trikona are Moon only.
Planets in upchaya house Ketu only. Planets in trik houses are Ketu, Mercury, Jupiter, Mars, and Rahu.

Directions in a natal chart

Below are the directions in a natal chart:

I - East (Sun is lord of East)

VII - West (Saturn)

IV- North (Mercury)

X- South (Mars)

XI & XII - South East (Venus)

VIII & IX - South West (Rahu)

II & III - North East (Jupiter)

V & VI - North West(Moon)

Therefore for Zaddy, his East will be Taurus, West is Scorpio, North is Leo and South is Aquarius. South East is Pisces and Aries. South west becomes Sagittarius and Capricorn. North East becomes Gemini and Cancer. North West becomes Virgo and Libra.

Significance of twelve houses

These twelve houses have different significations, such as

I - self

II- speech, wealth, etc.

III- brothers and sisters, communication, etc.

IV- mother, relatives, house, land, etc.

V- children, knowledge, primary learning, creativity, etc.

VI-debts, enemies, obstacles, etc.

VII- spouse, partner, partnership, etc.

VIII- longevity, hidden enemies, etc.

IX- fortunes, father, religion, higher learning, etc.

X- profession(livelihood), royalty, fame, etc.

XI- income, gains, pets, etc.

XII- expenses, isolation, losses, etc.

Body limbs and different houses

The limbs represented by different houses are as follows:

I- head (top portion), face

II- face, neck, right eye, right ear, right feet.

III-upper portion of chest and arms

IV-heart, breasts, portion above the stomach

V- stomach, the portion above the navel.

VI-portion below the navel and above the abdomen.

VII- below abdomen (navel and genitals)

VIII- genitals, anus.

IX-thighs, hips.

X- knees and back.

XI- calves, ankles.

XII- left feet, left eye, left ear.

The right side of the body consists of (half of I, II, III, IV, V, VI, and half of VII) and the left side of the body consists of (half of I, XII, XI, X, IX, VIII, and half of VII). It is symmetrical on both sides. When a child is born, first the left side is formed, then the right side is born in symmetry.

Sun is a natural significator of bones, Moon is of blood, Mars is of marrow, Mercury is of skin, Jupiter is of fat, Venus is of semen, and Saturn is of muscles, respectively.

Chapter 3

Planetary motion

All planets move in an anti-clockwise direction except the nodes Rahu and Ketu, which move in a retrograde or clockwise direction.

When a planet is marked as retrograde, it is usually represented by a dash "-" above the symbol or subscript "$_R$".

When planets such as Mars, Venus, Mercury, Jupiter and Saturn have a dash over its symbol in the natal chart, it notifies that planet is in retrograde motion for that particular birth chart. Retrograde planets appear to be moving in opposite directions when we observe them from the Earth. However, in reality, it doesn't happen. But in Jyotisha, retrograde planets have three additional effects as below:

A) It gives the result of the house it is positioned in as well as the house adjacent to it. So, say Mars is retrograde and placed in the III house. It will give the results of both II and III houses. It is like looking back and finishing the job that was started.

B) A retrograde planet will always be stronger than its natural state.

C) If the day one is born and the same planet is retrograde in the birth chart, it has a special significance with life path which we will discover as we progress through this book. For the moment consider, that a native is born on Tuesday (Mars) and his Mars is retrograde in his birth chart. So Mars becomes very special to him.

Planetary aspects

Each planet aspect the opposite house(seventh aspect) but Saturn, Mars, and Jupiter have extra aspects.

Sun aspect seventh from itself and illuminates the opposite house. The house where the sun sits loses some significance other than its own house, mooltrikona, and exaltation.

Moon aspect the seventh house as a reflection. The position of the Moon is the source of desire and the opposite house is where it requires reflection to fulfill the desire. Exceptions are exaltation and mooltrikona.

Mars aspect fourth, seventh, and eighth from itself. Mars is the son of the soil and a soldier, therefore it has a duty to protect its homeland, hence it always looks fourth from itself and therefore the fourth aspect. Mars's eighth aspect is destructive and transformative, it's death and re-birth. So, wherever Mars's eighth aspect falls, it is destructive. Mars's seventh aspect is always competition or chase.

Jupiter's aspect are fifth, seventh, and ninth from itself. Jupiter is the Jeeva karaka (living beings) and significator of progeny. It aspects fifth from itself because the fifth house of the cosmic man chart is progeny. Hence the fifth aspect. Also, Jupiter's dharma is that of a Brahmin who teaches and guides others. The ninth house of the cosmic man's chart represents dharma and guidance. Therefore, Jupiter gets the ninth aspect from itself as guidance and teaching. The position where Jupiter sits it expands.

Saturn's aspect is third, seventh, and tenth from itself. Saturn is an old taskmaster, significator ("karaka") of karma and he is neutral. For Saturn, it is always black and white and not grey. This old man, when gives his side eye (third aspect from itself), always brings destruction. It is like the taskmaster is looking through his shade for a cheating student. This gaze has its roots in the myth of Saturn, a curse given by his wife for not paying attention to her. The seventh aspect of Saturn humbles that house or breaks the ego. It is because the Sun gets debilitated in the seventh house in the sign of Libra in the cosmic man's chart. Hence, the seventh aspect of Saturn breaks ego. The tenth aspect of Saturn is karma or hard work. It is neutral, so as much as effort is put in, equivalent results will be obtained. In cosmic man's chart, tenth house is of Capricorn, which is livelihood or karma. Hence the tenth aspect.

Venus aspect seventh from itself. Its aspect is always for beauty, and superficiality. The house Venus sits in brings charm to it.

Rahu takes the aspect of the lord of the house it is sitting in. If Rahu is in Aries it will shape-shift into Mars and therefore have the aspect as fourth, seventh, and eighth. If it is in Sagittarius or Pisces then it will have fifth, seventh, and ninth aspects similar to that of Jupiter. When placed in Capricorn and Aquarius it will have a third, seventh, and tenth aspect similar to that of Saturn. If Rahu is sitting with either the Moon or Sun alone then it will not have any aspect but it will eclipse the luminaries thereby decreasing the strength of the Moon and the strength of the Sun respectively.

Ketu doesn't have eyesight because it doesn't have a body but it has intuitive skills. With those skills, it assumes the aspect of the planet in conjunction with it. Otherwise, it doesn't have any aspect. For all other positions, will affect only the house it sits in. If there are multiple planets in conjunction with Ketu it will take the aspect of the strongest planet.

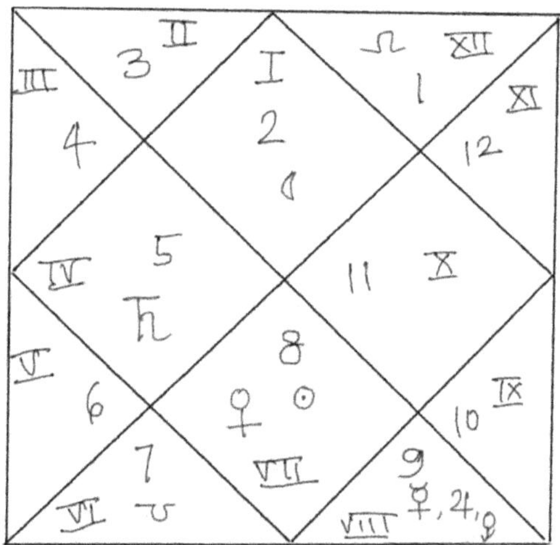

Now, take a look at Zaddy's natal chart and find out the different aspects of planets.

Moon is in the first house, therefore aspecting the seventh house and aspects fall on planets Venus and Sun as well. Sun and Venus also aspect seventh from itself therefore, it falls on the first house on the Moon as well.
Saturn is in the fourth house, so its third aspect from itself falls on the sixth house and Ketu. Its seventh aspect falls on the tenth house (Aquarius). Its tenth aspect from itself falls on the first house (Taurus) and Moon.

Mars's fourth aspect from itself falls on the XI house (Pisces). Its seventh aspect from itself falls on the II house (Gemini). Its eighth aspect from itself falls on III house (Cancer).

Mercury's seventh aspect from itself falls on II house (Gemini).

Jupiter's fifth aspect from itself falls on the XIII house (Aries) and on Rahu. Its seventh aspect falls on II house (Gemini). Its ninth aspect falls on the IV house (Leo).

Rahu is in the sign of Aries in the XII house. Aries' lord is Mars. So, Rahu shape-shifts into Mars and takes its fourth, seventh, and eighth aspects. The fourth aspect falls on the III house (Cancer), the seventh falls on the VI house (Libra) on Ketu, the eighth aspect falls on the VII house (Scorpio) and on Venus and Sun.

Ketu is in the sign of Libra in VI house. It will not have any aspect, only influences the VI house.

Chapter 4

Moon's position and respective desires

Moon in first house - desire of self, attention to self, physical appearance.

Second house- wealth, values, face, speech.

Third house- skills, communication.

Fourth house- stability, convenience, nurturer.

Fifth house- creativity, kids.

Sixth house- competition, work.

Seventh house- partnership, opposite gender.

Eighth house- occult, sex, mysticism.

Ninth house- foreign, religion, philosophy, higher learning.

Tenth house- status, fame, power.

Eleventh house- gains, network, social life, followers.

Twelfth house- sleep, bedroom, travel, isolation.

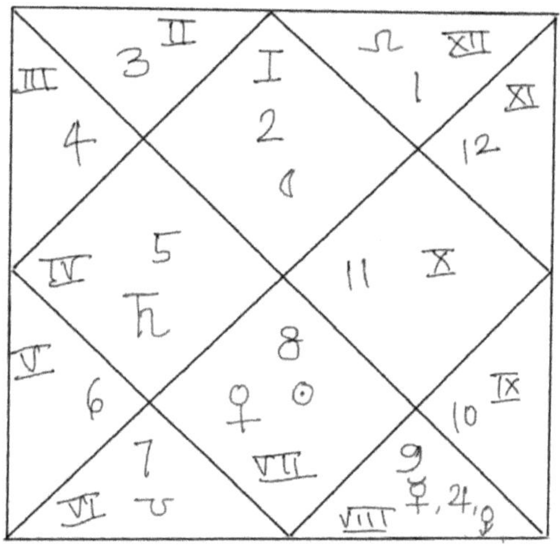

Here in Zaddy's chart, we see Moon is in the first house in the sign of Taurus (exaltation). Therefore, his desire is self. He wants the attention to himself and from the opposite house. Now, the opposite house has Venus as well as the Sun. Sun will burn wherever it is positioned and with Venus, it will either combust it or burn some significance of Venus as well. So, Zaddy will get the attention of the opposite gender, as Venus represents a female in a male's chart. But Saturn is always playing a spoiled sport in this, its tenth aspect falls on the Moon. Saturn's tenth aspect is for karma and heavy efforts. So despite Moon being exalted in lagna for Zaddy, he will still need to put a lot of effort into being the center of attention. Say, Saturn's aspect was not there, then it would have been a cakewalk for him with the rest two placements.

Planets and colours

Sun is copper or orange, Mars is deep red, Jupiter is yellow, Mercury is green, Saturn is dark blue, Venus is silver or luxurious and variegated, Moon is white, Rahu is black or smoky or uniquely variegated, Ketu is brown.

Whenever two planets are in conjunction they will create a mix of colours. For example, Mars+Jupiter will create Red+Yellow= Orange. Saturn+Mercury will create Blue+Green = Cyan. When the Moon is in conjunction with or receiving aspects from any planet, the native will be attracted to such colours by default. So if your favourite colour is red or a shade of red on the colour wheel. Then Moon is receiving aspects of Mars. If multiple planets are aspecting the moon then the strongest planet will determine your favourite colour or vice-versa. To determine the strongest of your planets take the colours of the planet which are in conjunction or aspecting the moon, mix them and witness what colour hues are obtained. The one that you like the most or the shade that you like the most is the planet that has strongest influence over the Moon in all of them. If this exercise is not done then one has to calculate numerous steps for the strength of a planet as there are positional strength or "sthan bala", directional strength or "dig bala" etc. It is beyond the scope of the book due to its complexity. The same method can be applied to different bhava which have other planets or aspects from those planets. You will observe the same colours either working for you (if they are supporting the chart) or working against you(if they are working against the chart). So if you want to paint the interiors of your home or building, you know that the fourth house in the natal chart represents that. Hence the colour can be as per your planetary aspect to the fourth house.

Chapter 5

Understanding Lagna and overall body

Ascendant determines the exoskeleton structure of the entire body and different planets in different houses add features to the respective limb either internally or externally.

Any mole or scar on the body is an indicator of the planets or conjunction of planets in the said house. Moles in the front side of the body are neutral or auspicious. Moles on the back side of the body are always inauspicious. Scars are also a mark of memory carried over lifetimes. If the mole is beautiful it is Mars or the Sun, if the skin has a blemish then Mercury is afflicted, and Ketu will give cuts and bruises to the aforesaid limb. If Jupiter is healthy it will give fat sometime excess. A strong Saturn will give strong stamina and determination while a weak one will make you lazy. A waxing moon gives a round-face or contour. A well-positioned Mercury will make one youthful and younger than their age. Planets will reflect their effects on the body, mind, and soul. Even smell, taste, or speech will reflect in a person's attributes. Before you begin to read your chart you must verify your birth time and ascendant. The planets will give the below effects to the limb in their natural state.

Sun- glamorous, well proportioned, great to look at, brightest.

Moon - soft, liquid, jovial.

Mars- small, red, contoured.

Mercury- small, younger, slim, duality, twins.

Jupiter- big, fat, short.

Venus- beauty, dusky, virile.

Saturn- long, dry, dark, ripped.

Rahu- marks, blemishes, tattoo marks.

Ketu- Cuts, deformity, holes, surgery marks.

Check your planets in the fourth house in your natal chart and the lord of the fourth house as well. Fourth lord conjunction with different planets.

Sun- strong, dry.

Moon- soft, standard.

Mars- small, reddish.

Mercury- very small, flat chest, micro.

Jupiter- big.

Venus- beautiful, dusky.

Saturn- dry, hard, elongated.

Different conjunctions create different effects in their natural state as follows:

Moon+Jupiter - big, curvaceous, Moon + Saturn - long, hard, Moon+Mars- standard,
Sun+Moon- bright, dry, Mercury+Moon - small, pulp, Venus+Moon - very beautiful, contoured. Mars + Jupiter - big and virile, Jupiter+Venus - big and beautiful. Jupiter+Saturn - huge. Jupiter+Saturn+Mars+Venus- big, huge, legendary. Saturn+Mars- long and active.

Conjunction effects are observed more closely as compared to planetary aspects. However, strong aspects such as Mars's fourth aspect and eighth aspect. Jupiter's ninth and fifth aspect and Saturn's third and tenth aspects can also change the size of the limb of the respective house.

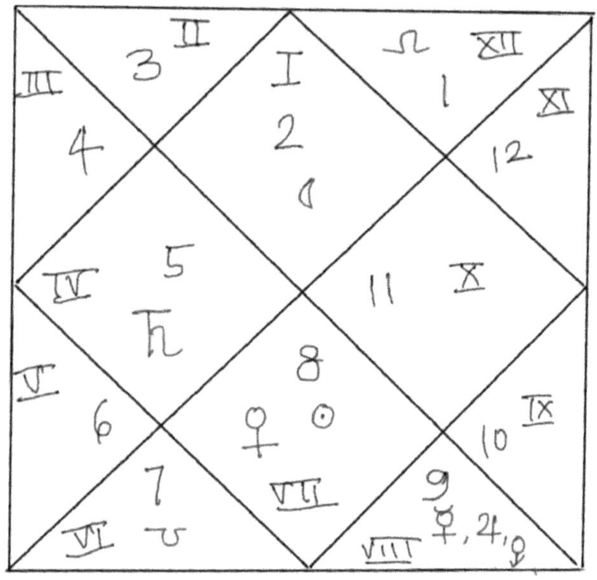

Let us check the above method in Zaddy's chart:

Ascendant lord Venus is in the seventh house but with the Sun. Venus is in Scorpio whose lord is Mars. Venus and Mars have a neutral relationship (neither enemy nor friend). However, Venus is with the enemy Sun. Also Sun despite being weak in strength due to being positioned in the west direction(VII house) will still burn some significance of Venus. In other words, it weakens Venus, but the aspect of the exalted Moon will be grace for Zaddy's appearance. He should have a face similar to a full Moon with subtle Venusian features also a glow due to the seventh aspect of Sun on the ascendant and a matured look due to the tenth aspect of Saturn.

Planetary taste

Different planets are assigned different taste.

☉ - pungent

☾ - saline

♂ - bitter

☿ - mixed

♃ - sweet

♀ - acidic

♄ - astringent

☊ - foreign

☋ - leftover

Now, recall Zaddy's chart. His II house lord is Mercury and placed in the VIII house with Mars and Jupiter. Therefore, the stronger of the planets will give him his favourite food taste. Since Jupiter is in his mooltrikona rashi, it is strong here. Therefore, Zaddy would like sweets. Mercury will give him a variety of sweets to taste.

Say, in the same above case, if Rahu were to be involved then he will like sweets of foreign origin i.e., of different culture or ethnicity. If Ketu were connected, then leftover foods are denoted. It doesn't mean that the native will be a beggar. It could be possible if the overall chart and life path denote penury. In other cases, either the native will leave food on the plate or someone from the family or respective house will share their leftover food so that it doesn't go to waste. We always have two people at any food court party, one who can't finish his plate and another foodie champion who aids others by finishing off their food as well.

Note: The above method will also help in rectifying the ascendant and verifying the birth time by noticing food habits.

Potential of a house in lagna(D1) Chart

The potential of a house is the number of possibilities it can offer. It is computed as below:

2^n (read as two to the power 'n') or simply means 2 multiplied n times, where n is the number of planets in that house or receiving aspect on that house and planet Mercury is involved either by aspect or by position.

OR

2^{n-1} where n is the number of planets in that house or receiving aspect on that house, excluding Mercury.

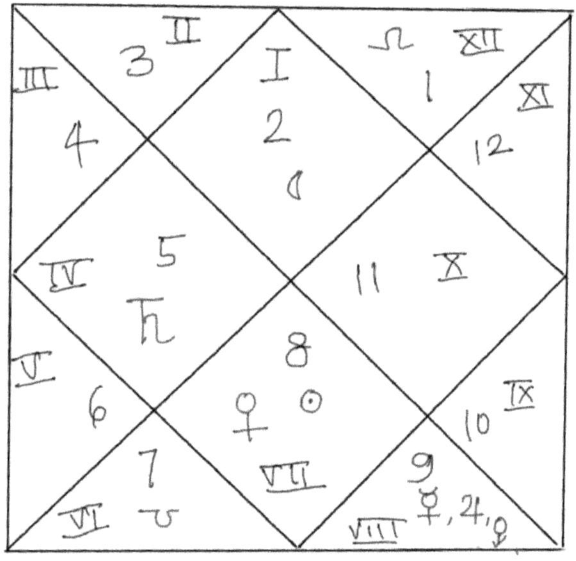

Let us check the potential for II house in Zaddy's chart. II house is receiving aspects from Mercury, Mars, and Jupiter. Since Mercury is involved, the formula we use is 2^n, $n = 3$, so $2^3 = 8$. Therefore, eight possibilities exist for the second house. Now second house signifies vocal chords, speech, wealth, etc. Therefore, Zaddy's chart has a promise that he can speak eight different languages or eight different voice modulations, eight different forms of wealth. These possibilities can become true if D1 and D60 are coherent, or multiply if D1, D9, D60 all are coherent, or diminish if D1 and D60 are incoherent. This will require a lot more understanding, which we will develop as we progress.

Similarly, the III house has two possibilities of skillset. It is because of the eighth aspect of Mars on the III house and the fourth aspect from Rahu. So n=2, $2^{n-1} = 2$.

Similarly, his seventh house has a potential of $2^{n-1} = 8$ (here n=4, Moon, Venus, Sun, and Rahu involvement), which relates to the possibilities of eight marriages or business partnership, relations, etc. When this same method is applied to the Moon rather than a house, it gives the possibilities of personalities one person can have. So, if Zaddy chooses to be an actor then his Moon has ($2^{3-1} = 4$) four possible characters to play. In the world of psychology, sometimes it can also be referred to as multiple personalities. In occult, it is called shape-shifting.

Sourabh Roy

Chapter 6

Zodiac span and degrees

The entire zodiac span is considered 360 degrees. Each zodiac sign is 30 degrees so twelve zodiac signs give 12x30 =360 degrees. Similarly, each house is considered 30 degrees for easier calculation even though when observed some zodiac signs are less than 30 degrees and few are greater than 30 degrees.

Divisional charts

In Brihat Parasara Hora Shastra, sixteen divisional charts are being referred to. "Amsa" means division. The following are different divisional charts:

D1- Ascendant or Lagna.

D2- Hora for wealth.

D3- Drekkana for co-born.

D4- Chaturthamsa for fortunes.

D7- Progeny.

D9- Navamsa for spouse or luck.

D10- Dasamsa for power and position (livelihood etc).

D12- Dwadamsa for parents.

D16- Shodamsa for conveyances.

D20- Bisamsa for worship, spiritual progress, etc.

D24- Chaturbisamsa for academic achievements.

D27- Bhamsa or Nakshatramsa for strength and weakness.

D30- Trisamsa for evils.

D40- Khavedamsa for auspicious and inauspicious effects.

D45- Akshavedamsa for all general indications

D60- Shastiamsa for all general indications and past life.

Each divisional chart has a set of methods for its computation. We will understand how it is calculated for a few charts. However, we will focus majorly on D1, D9 and D60.

Computing D2 or Hora Chart

As the number 2 suggests it will have two divisions of a sign. If a sign is 30 degrees. Then each division becomes 15 degrees. But, each divisional chart gets a deity or an owner for that division. Consider, an apartment which is the zodiac sign. Now that apartment is owned by the respective planet. So if the zodiac sign is Aries, lord Mars is the owner of the entire apartment. However, inside the apartment, there are many blocks for different tenants. So, it is the ownership of that tenant to take care of that block even if he gets another sub-tenant in that block. Here, in D2 the two block owners are Sun and Moon. The first half(15 degrees) of the odd sign is ruled by the Sun and the second half(15 degrees) is ruled by the Moon. The reverse order applies to even signs.

Odd signs are Aries, Gemini, Leo, Libra, Sagittarius, Aquarius.

Even signs are Taurus, Cancer, Virgo, Scorpio, Capricorn, Pisces.

Sign	Hora lord(0°-15°)	Hora lord(15° -30°)
Aries	Sun	Moon
Taurus	Moon	Sun
Gemini	Sun	Moon
Cancer	Moon	Sun
Leo	Sun	Moon
Virgo	Moon	Sun
Libra	Sun	Moon
Scorpio	Moon	Sun
Sagittarius	Sun	Moon
Capricorn	Moon	Sun

Sign	Hora lord(0º-15º)	Hora lord(15º -30º)
Aquarius	Sun	Moon
Pisces	Moon	Sun

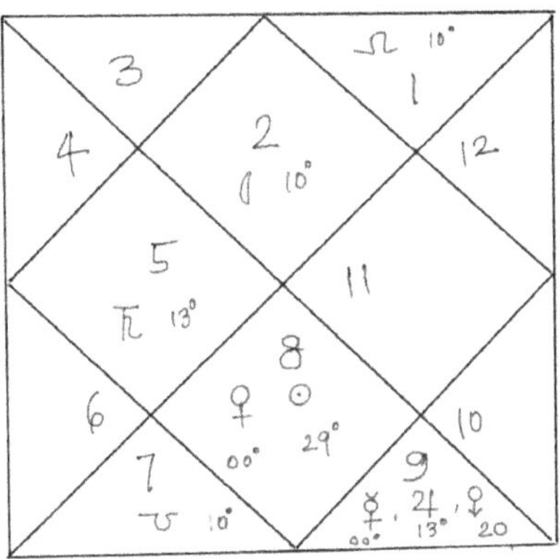

Now, we apply this on Zaddy's chart to compute the D2, Hora chart.

Moon is 10 degrees in the sign of Taurus which is an even sign therefore Moon will go under lordship of its own in D2 chart.

Saturn is 13 degrees in the sign of Leo which is an odd sign therefore hora lord becomes the Sun.

Venus is 0 degrees in even sign Scorpio so it falls under lordship of Moon.

Sun is 29degrees in even sign so it falls under the lordship of Sun(its own).

Mars is 20 degrees in odd sign so it falls under the lordship of Moon.

Jupiter is 13 degrees in odd sign so it falls under the lordship of the Sun.

Mercury is 0 degrees in odd sign so it falls under the lordship of the Sun.

Rahu and Ketu each are in the odd sign and 10 degrees, so fall under the lordship of the Sun.

Therefore, in D2 chart, under the lordship of Sun, we have planets (Saturn, Rahu, Ketu, Mercury, Jupiter, Sun) and under the lordship of Moon we have planets (Moon, Venus, Mars).

Note: There is no concept of houses or bhavas in any divisional chart, only lordship. Hence, we should not read any divisional chart the way we read D1 or lagna chart.

Computing D9 or Navamsa chart

As the number 9 suggests, it will have ninth divisions (1/9th) of a sign. Therefore, 30 degrees divided by nine gives 3 degrees 20 minutes (3°20′) each. The navamsa calculation for a movable sign is from there itself and successive sign. For a fixed sign, it's ninth from itself and successive sign thereafter. For a dual sign, it is fifth from itself and successive sign thereafter. The below demonstrates this. M-movable, F- fixed, and D-dual signs, respectively.

Division	Aries(M)	Taurus (F)	Gemini(D)	Cancer(M)	Leo (F)	Virgo(D)	Libra(M)	Scorpio(F)	Sagittarius(D)	Capricorn(M)	Aquarius(F)	Pisces (D)
0 < 3°20′	1	10	7	4	1	10	7	4	1	10	1	4
3°20′ < 6°40′	2	11	8	5	2	11	8	5	2	11	8	5
6°40′ < 10°	3	12	9	6	3	12	9	6	3	12	9	6

Divisi on	Aries(M)	Tauru s(F)	Gemi ni(D)	Ca nc er(M)	Le o(F)	Vir go(D)	Lib ra(M)	Sc orp io(F)	Sa gitt ari us(D)	Ca pri cor n(M)	Aq uar ius (F)	Pis ces (D)
10º < 13º 20'	4	1	10	7	4	1	10	7	4	1	10	7
13º 20' < 16º 40'	5	2	11	8	5	2	11	8	5	2	11	8
16º 40' < 20º	6	3	12	9	6	3	12	9	6	3	12	9
20º < 23º 20'	7	4	1	10	7	4	1	10	7	4	1	10
23º 20' < 26º 40'	8	5	2	11	8	5	2	11	8	5	2	11
26º 40' < 30º	9	6	3	12	9	6	3	12	9	6	3	12

Now let us compute the navamsa chart for Zaddy.

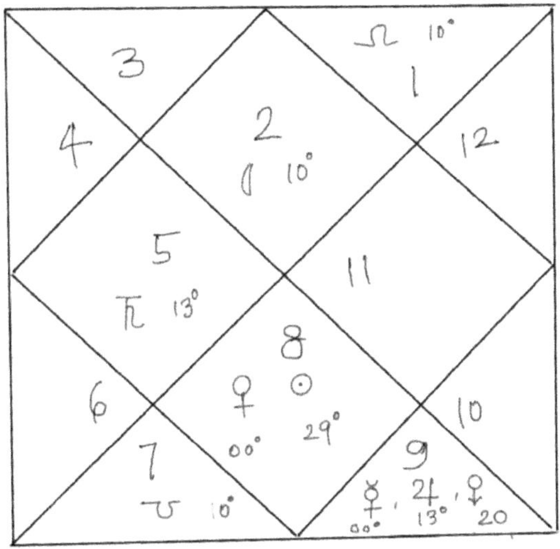

D1 chart

Moon is 10° in Taurus. Taurus is a fixed sign, so the first division will be ninth from itself, so counting nine places from Taurus gives us Capricorn. And the second division (3°20' - 6°40') will fall in Aquarius and so forth. Moon's degree is 10, so it falls in Aries navamsa.

Ascendant is at 8° in Taurus so it will fall in Pisces navamsa.

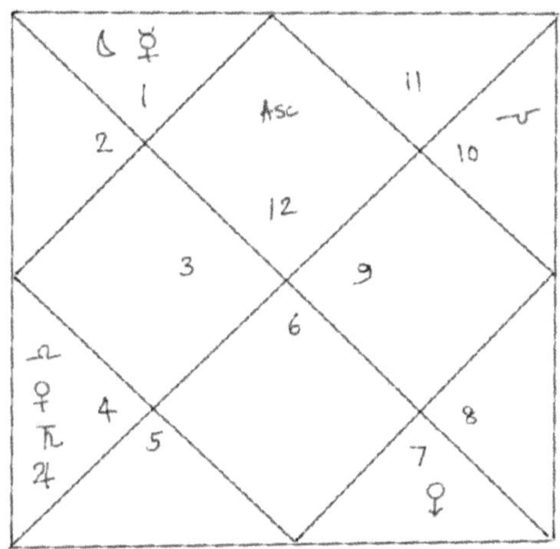

Refer to the above table and degree span for other planets.

D9 chart

Saturn's degree is 13º in Leo(F) and falls in Cancer navamsa.

Venus is 0º in Scorpio(F) and therefore falls in Cancer navamsa.

Sun is 29º in Scorpio(F) and therefore falls in Pisces navamsa.

Mercury is 0º in Sagittarius, which is a dual sign. Therefore, its first division will be fifth from itself. Five places from Sagittarius give us Aries. So Mercury will fall in Aries navamsa.

Jupiter is 13º in Sagittarius(D) and therefore falls in Cancer navamsa.

Mars is 20º in Sagittarius(D) and therefore falls in Libra navamsa.

Rahu is 10º in Aries(M) therefore, the first division will be computed from Aries itself. Since the degree is 10 therefore it falls in Cancer navamsa.

Ketu is 10º in Libra(M) and therefore falls in Capricorn navamsa.

Exercise: We have calculated the D9 chart for Zaddy as above. Calculate D9 for your natal chart.

Computing D60 or Shastiamsa chart

As the number 60 suggests, it will be the sixtieth (1/60th) division of a sign. Therefore, 30 degrees divided by 60 gives us 30 minutes. To calculate the shastiamsa, we only consider the degree of the planet. Multiply the degree of the planet by 2 and then divide it by 12. Add 1 to the remainder to find which sign the shastiamsa falls. For example, Saturn is 13º23′ in Leo. So multiply 13º23′ x 2 = 26º46′. Now ignore the minutes, take the degree 26, and divide by 12. It gives the remainder as 2. Add 1 to the remainder, so 2+1= 3. Now, the shastiamsa will fall three signs from Leo, which is Libra. Therefore, Saturn goes into the shastiamsa of Libra. Now, each shastiamsa has a lordship as below for even and odd signs. '**M**' stands for malefic shastiamsa and '**B**' stands for beneficial shastiamsa. If a planet is in beneficial shastiamsa, then the house owned by that planet in the D1 chart is beneficial to the planet. If it's in malefic shastiamsa, the house owned by the planet in the D1 chart suffers from a defect.

Natural benefic planets are waxing Moon, Jupiter, Venus, and Mercury alone. Natural malefic planets are Sun, Mars, Saturn, Rahu, Ketu, waning Moon.

If a benefic planet falls in a beneficial shastiamsa the houses give good results. If a benefic planet falls in malefic shastiamsa the house gives bad results. A malefic planet will always give malefic results but intensity would be reduced if it falls in beneficial shastiamsa.

Consider the table below.

Odd sign	Shastiamsa lordship	Even sign
0º < 0º 30'	Ghora(M)- extreme.	29º 30' < 30º
0º30' < 1º	Raksha(M)- demon, evil.	29º < 29º30'
1º < 1º30'	Deva(B)- divine, spiritual side.	28º30' < 29º
1º30' < 2º	Kubera(B)- celestial treasurer.	28º < 28º30'
2º < 2º 30'	Yaksha(B)- celestial singer.	27º30' < 28º
2º 30' < 3º	Kinnara(B)- a deformed man, a mythical being with human head on a horse.	27º < 27º30'
3º < 3º 30'	Bhrasta(M)- fallen, vicious.	26º30' < 27º
3º 30' < 4º	Kulaghna(M)- ruining name of family lineage.	26º < 26º30'
4º < 4º 30'	Garala(M)- poison or venom.	25º30' < 26º
4º 30' < 5º	Vahini(M)- fire, gastric fluid, digestive faculty, appetite.	25º < 25º30'
5º < 5º 30'	Maya(M)- deceit, jugglery.	24º30' < 25º

Odd sign	Shastiamsa lordship	Even sign
5o 30' < 6o	Purishaka(M)- dirt.	24o < 24o30'
6o < 6o30'	Apampathi(B)- the ocean, Varuna, (the rain god).	23o30' < 24o
6o30' < 7o	Marut(B)- wind god.	23o < 23o30'
7o < 7o 30'	Kaala(M)- dark blue colour, weather, Saturn, Siva's personification of destructive principle.	22o30' < 23o
7o 30' < 8o	Sarpa(M)- snake.	22o < 22o30'
8o < 8o30'	Amrita(B)-immortal, nectar.	21o30' < 22o
8o30' < 9o	Indu(B)- Moon, the number 1, camphor.	21o < 21o30'
9o < 9o30'	Mridu(B) - moderate, soft.	20o30' < 21o
9o30' < 10o	Komala(B)- tender, agreeable.	20o < 20o30'
10o < 10o30'	Heramba(B)- Ganesha, a boastful hero, buffalo.	19o30' < 20o
10o30' < 11o	Brahma(B)- the Universal father, sacred knowledge.	19o < 19o30'

Odd sign	Shastiamsa lordship	Even sign
11º < 11º30'	Vishnu(B)-the second deity of the sacred triad, name of Agni, a pious man, name of a lawgiver.	18º30' < 19º
11º30' < 12º	Maheswara(B)- the third deity of the Triad ensuring task of destruction.	18º < 18º30'
12º < 12º30'	Deva(B)- divine, spiritual side.	17º30' < 18º
12º30' < 13º	Ardra(B)-moist.	17º < 17º30'
13º < 13º30'	Kalinasa(M)- destruction of strife.	16º30' < 17º
13º30' < 14º	Kshiteesa(B)-ruler of earth.	16º < 16º30'
14º < 14º30'	Kamalakara(B)- a lake full of lotuses, an assemblage of lotuses.	15º30' < 16º
14º30' < 15º	Gulika(M)-son of Saturn.	15º < 15º30'
15º < 15º30'	Mrithyu(M)- son of Mars, death.	14º30' < 15º
15º30' < 16º	Kaala(M)- dark blue colour, weather, Saturn, Siva's personification of destructive principle.	14º < 14º30'

Odd sign	Shastiamsa lordship	Even sign
16º < 16º30'	Davagani(M)- a forest conflagration.	13º30' < 14º
16º30' < 17º	Ghora(M)- extreme.	13º < 13º30'
17º < 17º30	Yama(M)- death personified.	12º30' < 13º
17º30' < 18º	Kanataka(M)-thorn, any trouble-some fellow to the state, enemy of the order and government.	12º < 12º30'
18º < 18º30'	Sudha(B)- nectar, ambrosia, name of the Ganges.	11º30' < 12º
18º30' < 19º	Amrita(B)-immortal, nectar.	11º < 11º30'
19º < 19º30'	Poornachandra(B)- Full moon.	10º30' < 11º
19º30' < 20º	Vishadagdha(M)- destroyed by venom, consumed by grief.	10º < 10º30'
20º < 20º30'	Kulnasa(M)- destruction of	9º30' < 10º
20º30' < 21º	Vamsakshaya(M)-not growing further.	9º < 9º30'
21º < 21º30'	Utpata(M)- a portentous or unusual phenomenon, earthquake, eclipses,	8º30' < 9º

Odd sign	Shastiamsa lordship	Even sign
21°30' < 22°	Kaala(M)- dark blue colour, weather, Saturn, Siva's personification of destructive principle.	8° < 8°30'
22° < 22°30'	Saumya(B)- relating or sacred to Moon, handsome, auspicious.	7° 30' < 8°
22°30' < 23°	Komala(B)- tender, agreeable.	7° < 7° 30'
23° < 23°30'	Seetala(B)- cold, Moon, camphor, sandal, turpentine.	6°30' < 7°
23°30' < 24°	Karaladamshtra(M)- frightful teethed.	6° < 6°30'
24° < 24°30'	Chandramukhi(B)- having the beauty of the Moon.	5° 30' < 6°
24°30' < 25°	Praveena(B)-clever, versed in.	5° < 5° 30'
25° < 25°30'	Kala Pavaka(M)- the destructive fire at the end of the world.	4° 30' < 5°
25°30' < 26°	Dandayudha(M)- the staff held by an ascetic(or by a Bhramin)	4° < 4° 30'

Odd sign	Shastiamsa lordship	Even sign
26º < 26º30'	Nirmala(B)- resplendent, sinless, stainless, virtuous.	3º 30' < 4º
26º30' < 27º	Saumya(B)- relating or sacred to Moon, handsome, auspicious.	3º < 3º 30'
27º < 27º30'	Kroora(M)- pitiless, mischievous, bloody, terrible.	2º 30' < 3º
27º30' < 28º	Atiseetala(B)- very cold.	2º < 2º 30'
28º < 28º30'	Amrita(B)-immortal, nectar.	1º30' < 2º
28º30' < 29º	Payodhi(B)- Ocean.	1º < 1º30'
29º < 29º30'	Bhramana(M)- wandering.	0º30' < 1º
29º 30' < 30º	Chandrarekha(B)- streak of the moon.	0º < 0º 30'

You can either compute the D60 chart for each planet or you can use the software and check it.

How to use the above table. Look at the D1 chart of Zaddy, his ascendant lord Venus is 0º in Scorpio(even sign), therefore check the table under the even sign column and look for degree 0. The corresponding shastiamsa lord is chandrarekha(B). It is benefic shastiamsa and Venus is a natural benefic. So the houses owned by Venus in his chart will have beneficial effects. Taurus and Libra are the signs owned by Venus, in his chart Taurus is the first house and Libra is the sixth house. Moon is in the first house in exaltation. So we can say Zaddy should have a very attractive physique. If that is not the case then we need to verify other parameters to make sure we reach the exact birth time.

His ninth and tenth lord is Saturn, which is 13º in Leo(odd sign) therefore the shastiamsa lordship will be Kalinasa(M). Saturn is a malefic planet and falls in malefic shastiamsa, therefore the ninth and tenth house suffers a defect.

If a different benefic planet either sits in a defected house or aspect it. It acts as a saving grace for that house and some malefic effects are reduced. Contrarily can be said about a malefic planet which will make it worse.

Now, there is a separate method to read a D60 chart on its own, which involves a bit of advanced understanding and is beyond the scope of this book.

We need D60 because, any promise in the D1 chart when blocked in D60 will not fructify. If any promise is there in D1 but, D9 is incoherent, D60 is supportive, then it will fructify. If any theme is not in the D1 chart but present in D9 and D60, it will still fructify. If a promise is in the D1 chart as well as D9 but not supported by D60, it will fail to fructify. In other words, if D1, D9, and D60 all three are coherent, it make an extraordinary chart, whether for better or worse for the native is a different story. If D1, D9 and D60 all are divergent, then the chart is extremely unfortunate. These two are extreme conditions and are very rarely observed, for most people, their fate lies somewhere in between.

Chapter 7

Lordship of Shastiamsa

All the benefic shastiamsa induces artistic quality, all malefic shastiamsa includes mechanical or technical qualities. The same shastiamsa lordship can produce different results for a different person, it is because there are Rashi(sign), bhavas, nakshatras, padas, and the overall chart varies at the D60 level.

Example 1:

Kulaghna(M) shastiamsa, means which brings bad name to family lineage. In cosmic man's chart lineage is IX house. So going against the values of the ninth house is called Kulaghna. But, when a planet owns a different house in D1 chart other than IX house, then this should be applied judiciously. In such a scenario it will be the value system for the house which has been discarded.

In the epic Mahabharata, there was a moment when Subhadra kidnaps Arjuna to wed him. It was a planned event under the instruction of Sri Krishna but for that event Arjuna became kulaghna, it is because he hailed from a clan of

Kshatriya(warriors) whose dharma is to battle, and if such a fierce warrior like him is kidnapped by a damsel it does go against the trait of a Kshatriya.

Similarly, in the epic Ramayana, Vibhishana betrayed his brother Ravana because he went against the lineage. We find the same stories over and over again, another example is Prahalad. He was an ardent devotee of lord Vishnu but his father didn't acknowledge Vishnu. Prahalad could have walked into his father's shoes but he didn't therefore he was a Kulaghna for his lineage as well.

Say, in the D1 chart, a native's tenth lord is in Kulaghna shastiamsa, so his profession could be extremely different than his family lineage. Say, the entire family are a lineage of technocrats but the child became a musician which doesn't bode well with the parents. Or say the parents were teachers but the native became a sex worker.

So, the same shastiamsa lordship can create an array of possibilities depending upon house, rashi, and nakshatras.

Example 2: Heramba(B) shastiamsa refers to the story of Lord Ganesha. It is also known as the shastiamsa of numero uno. The reason lies in the story of Ganesha itself. He was born from Shakti (a form of Goddess Parvati), with siddhi by birth. But, no one can attain siddhi without earning it. The laws of nature apply to mortals, devas, and Gods as well, such is ordained by the supreme consciousness. Hence, when Maheswara(a form of lord Shiva) chopped off Ganesha's head and replaced it with a big brain, Ganesha as a child was crying and inconsolable, to alleviate that; Maheswara gave him a blessing that he would be the one propitiated first before anyone else, and all other Gods agreed. Hence, whenever any God or Goddess is worshipped in India, lord Ganesha is propitiated firstly with "Om Ganeshaya Namah". Now, this story becomes the reason for being numero uno when connected with a particular house in a birth chart plus two more insights are gained from the story. Firstly because of his father, his head was chopped off or sacrificed. Secondly, he loved his mother more than his father because he was guarding the door at his mother's request. Prominent lead actors or actresses, sportspersons, politicians, diplomats, etc whatever may be the profession, will do top-notch work in that area. So, if this shastiamsa makes a connection with II and X house and the profession is that of a singer, the native has a promise in the D1 chart to become a top-notch in his field, rest his efforts will determine.

Interestingly, the fictional character Robin Hood's profession is also Heramba shastiamsa, he was a top-notch thief, stealing from the rich and giving it to the poor. On the other hand, if it connects with III and X house, it can give exceptional writing skills as well, whichever house is lorded by Heramba shastiamsa achieves excellence. The native can either become a top-notch thief, a leader, an actor, or writer, it will all vary from the involvement of different houses. If it makes a connection with your seventh house, then your spouse will be like a hero/heroine.

Example 3: Brahma(B) shastiamsa denotes skills of knowledge, it involves teachers, scholars, PhD holders, scientists, policymakers, etc. The respective house and house lord placed in Brahma shastiamsa will give such skills, if the native is not equipped then family members of such native could possess such skills.

There are few shastiamsa that result in barbarism, cruelty, gore, horror, brutality, etc. Those are beyond the scope of this book, but you can discover them at your own pace.

Consider that all the seven planets in your D1 chart fall into unique shastiamsa. And if any house has planets in conjunction or multiple aspects from other planets. Then a combination of Shastiamsa lordship will happen i.e., Brahma shastiamsa + Yaksha shastiamsa is there for the II and III house. Here, not only the native is a singer but also can teach others, therefore the native can be a motivational speaker as well.

The more the number of planets involved in a house, the more complex it will become, but as long as the story of the shastiamsa is known, one can conclude after a holistic approach to the entire chart. Below are a few shastiamsa that you can look into for case studies in your birth chart and apply **judiciously**.

Indu- aspect of goddess Parvati.

Davagani - a story of deity Agni, fire of anger.

Vahini - a story of Swaha; wife of Agni, fire of digestion.

Kalapavaka - children of Agni and Swaha, fire of carnal pleasure.

Gulika - son of Saturn.

Mrithyu - son of Mars.

Kaala - destructive side of lord Shiva.

Ghora - aspect of Indra.

Deva- court of Indra.

Kubera - deity, a treasurer of gold.

Yaksha - story of maidens in the court of Kubera.

Dandayudha - an aspect of sage Durvasa.

Purishaka - a story of nymph Urvasi.

Kamalakara - story of Saugandhika.

Maheswara - the story of lord Shiva before the birth of Ganesha.

Chandramukhi - aspect of Ganga.

Chandrarekha - story of Tara; wife of Brihaspati.

Poornachandra - aspect of nymph Urvashi.

Kalinasa - aspect of nymph Tilotama.

Bhramana - aspect of sage Parasara.

Maya - aspect of Indra.

Ardra - aspect of Ahalya, aspect of Ganga.

The story of shastiamsa lordship or any deity for that matter is present in Puranas or any other classical text either hidden or explicitly mentioned. To read these classical texts, one needs excellent proficiency and command over Sanskrit plus knowledge of planets and nakshatras. Here in the book, you are acquainted with the planets. Now, considering such a level of Sanskrit proficiency is not feasible for most people. Therefore, you can refer to translated works of such classics from revered translators and authors, get your hands on different publications of the same classic, and you will start to notice the difference. Although every writer has his own bias which is unavoidable, as a reader when you are equipped with planets and nakshatras you can decipher it well, this method can be applied across classics of different religions or lost civilisation with the help of subject matter experts for such classics.

If a comet or asteroid is falling, then the connection with Bhrasta shastiamsa can be mapped; it is self-explanatory. If extreme sports then ghora.

If cancer disease then Yama; Yama is the stepbrother of Saturn, as a child Yama kicked Chaaya, his stepmother, who cursed him that his leg would always be infected. To relieve Yama of pain, Saturn gave him a crow to eat those worms and relieve him of pain. Carcinoma cells always outgrow fast in the body, so we can witness the same theme of Yama with cancer disease, philosophers and occultists are also connected with Yama.

If Deva, Saumya, or Mridu are involved, then skills of singing or soft voice.

If Kaala shastiamsa is connected with Moon or Sun, then the presence of narcissism, damage of seed.

If Praveena then politician, salesman, astrologer, etc. These are a few examples of how to check and use them. It will get more clear in upcoming chapters.

Exercise: *Now, check your D1 chart and D60 lordship for each planet. Note them down. You have to search for those and apply them judiciously. Leverage your strength according to your chart. The story below can enlighten you.*

Story of a mouse called Maudib:

A small mouse was scared of cats, he witnessed a lot of his friends being eaten by cats. He prayed to God. 'Please God. Make me a cat'. God granted him his wish. He became a cat. Now, he witnessed the dogs hunting cats. So he prayed again, 'God, please God, one more time. Please make me a dog.' God granted his wish again. Now, he has become a dog. He witnessed the cows kicking the dogs and eating their food. He prayed again. 'God, I can't live like this. I want power, power. Please make me a Cow.' God granted his wish again, he became a cow. A few months went well, then when all the cows were taken by the herdsman to cross the river, they were all frantic. Now, Maudib wants to become a river. He asked for a wish again and got it granted. This time he became a river, flowing, splashing waves. During sunny days and extreme heat, he started to evaporate fast. Maudib saw Sun was even more powerful than him. He prayed again. 'God. Please, God, this time will be the last one, I promise.' God granted his wish again. He was a beaming ray of light and glowing, giving light to everybody. If he doesn't wake up people pray to him. But one day, a dark black cloud covered Maudib, it was lightning, cracking sounds, and thunderstorms. Maudib couldn't believe there was someone more powerful than the Sun until now. So he prayed again. 'God, dear dear God. Can you please squeeze a last wish for me? I want to become clouds.' God granted his wish again. And he became clouds. He was showing his thunder, a chariot of lightning everywhere. Then after travelling a lot of distance, he crashed into a mountain. He couldn't move past the mountain and started weeping and crying. Maudib prayed again, 'God, dear God, can you hear me? I want to become a Mountain.' God granted his wish again. Now, Maudib has become a Mountain, soaring high of the highest peak, stopping all clouds. A few years passed, and Maudib was very happy that he was the most powerful thing on Earth. Then he realised a small mouse had made numerous holes at its base, causing cracks, and crevices, resulting in landslides and cracking of the mountain. He was surprised, a mountain as big and powerful as him, his roots were shattered by a small mouse. Maudib realised his mistake. He prayed again. 'God, I want to return to be a mouse again.'

God spoke 'I thought you didn't want to be a mouse. Why the change of heart?'

'I never realised a mouse could possess such strength.'

'Are you sure you will not change your mind again?'

'No, I know for certain now. I wish to become a mouse.' God granted him his last wish and Maudib became a mouse again, happy in his own skin and realising his core strength.

Chapter 8

Consciousness of a child

When a child is born, the placement of Ketu will determine the year of his consciousness. Mostly, every child learns through imitation games by observing and imitating their surroundings or someone who teaches them. But it can't be denied that there are child prodigies who already knew by birth a few inherent traits no one taught them. It is Ketu and D60 chart that determines this phenomenon. If Ketu is in I house in the natal chart, the child will show immediate skills or traits of immediate past life right from the first year. If Ketu is in IV house, then the time taken by Ketu to travel from IV to I house will become the year of consciousness of the child. Ketu has to travel four houses(because it is always clockwise). On average the nodes take eighteen months to cross one house based on observation in the sky. Therefore to cross four houses, $4 \times 18 = 72$ months or 6th year. Therefore the consciousness for the above child will happen in 6th year. If Ketu is in III house then 4.5 years. Hence, consciousness will awaken between the age of 4 - 5. If Ketu is in the fifth house then around the age of 7 - 8. If Ketu is in the XII house then it will be around the age of 18.

These traits can also be observed in other children who may not be child prodigies, by their parents or people close to them on a very subtle level. This is an exceptional method for a native to rectify his own birth time because one can confirm those traits from near and dear ones and no one else will know.

Note: If you have made it this far, then you have the tools to make sure that your ascendant is correct, and your body features match with it.

Chapter 9

Yogas in birth chart

Yogas means combination(promise) in a natal chart. There are numerous yogas with respect to the ascendant, sign, Moon(lunar yogas), Sun(Solar yogas), and many miscellaneous yogas. We will not burden ourselves with so many numbers because we already know if the promise is there in D1, but denied in D60 it will not fructify. Two people born on the same day will possess the same natal chart, same planetary dasha yet results would be vastly different. If the yogas are fructifying in any birth chart it will reflect in the native or it will activate during respective planetary dasha. If an excellent promise is there in any chart but the dasha doesn't come, such yoga goes waste for the present birth. So, why know yogas at all? It is because one man can't change his fate but someone else can change that for him. If the other person's chart has supporting yogas then it will help the native as well. It is similar to a scenario, when you go to worship in a temple and put flowers at the feet of the deity, a few insects in the flower also go along with it and reach a place where even you are not allowed. Now, this is where the navamsa works. Which kind of person is going to help you with that can be determined through navamsa. Usually, an easy way to change fate is through marriage or partnership, and in most cases it does work but sometimes imitating societal patterns can also do damage.

In any natal chart, trikon(I, V, IX) and kendra(I, IV, VII, X) are very powerful houses. Any yoga forming through these has much more impact. Some yogas promise beneficial results to the native or neutralise malefic yoga and there are ones that give malefic results or cancel a promise.

Few yogas are worth discovering if at all one wants to look at. The lunar yogas are as kemadruma yoga, sunaphaa, anaphaa and duradhara, dhana yoga, adhi yoga. The solar yogas vesi, vosi and ubhayachara yoga. Miscellaneous yogas such as budhaditya yoga, pancha mahapurusha yoga, gajakesari yoga, amala yoga, guru mangal yoga, parvata yoga, brahma yoga, vishnu yoga, shiva yoga, dharmakarmadhipati yoga, vipareet rajayoga, etc.

Sourabh Roy

Gajakesari yoga

When Jupiter is in kendra (I, IV, VII, X) from the ascendant or from Moon, and is conjunct or aspected by another benefic, avoiding at the same time debilitation and inimical house, Gajakesari yoga is formed.

One born in this yoga will be splendorous, intelligent, endowed with many laudable virtues, and will please the king. 'Gaja' means elephant, 'Kesari' means lion. Therefore it is equivalent to royal status of Kings.

From the above we can say Jupiter can't be in Capricorn sign as well as Jupiter+Sun combustion is not allowed.

Jupiter in I, IV, VII, X from ascendant or Moon.

Jupiter should not be in an inimical house; to compute this we must know the relation of Jupiter with other planets.

Natural relationship

Planets	Friends	Enemies	Equals
Sun	Moon, Mars, Jupiter	Venus, Saturn	Mercury

Planets	Friends	Enemies	Equals
Moon	Sun, Mercury		Mars, Jupiter, Venus,
Mars	Sun, Moon, Jupiter	Mercury	Venus, Saturn
Mercury	Sun, Venus	Moon	Mars, Jupiter,
Jupiter	Sun, Moon, Mars	Mercury, Venus	Saturn
Venus	Mercury, Saturn	Moon, Sun	Mars, Jupiter
Saturn	Mercury, Venus	Sun, Moon, Mars	Jupiter

When we look at gajakesari yoga whether from ascendant or Moon, we have to look at the compound relationship.

Compound relationship = natural relationship + temporary relationship.

Sourabh Roy

Temporary relationship

The planet positioned in X, IV, XI, III, II, or XII from another becomes a mutual friend else enemies. This will vary depending on the chart.

Compound relationship

Natural relationship	Temporary relationship	Net relationship
Friends	Friends	Extreme friendship
Neutral	Friends	Friendship
Enemies	Enemies	Extreme enmity
Neutral	Enemies	Enemies
Enemies	Friends	Neutral

So, in Zaddy's chart, we have a temporary relationship as below:

Planets	Friends	Enemies
Sun	Mercury, Jupiter, Mars, Saturn	Venus, Moon
Moon	Saturn	Venus, Sun, Mercury, Jupiter, Mars
Mars	Sun, Venus	Mercury, Jupiter, Moon, Saturn
Mercury	Sun, Venus	Jupiter, Mars, Moon, Saturn
Jupiter	Sun, Venus	Mercury, Mars, Moon, Saturn
Venus	Saturn, Mercury, Mars, Jupiter	Sun, Moon
Saturn	Sun, Venus, Moon	Mercury, Jupiter, Mars

So, the compound relationship for Jupiter in the case of Zaddy is Sun-extreme friend, Moon- Neutral, Mars- Neutral, Mercury- Extreme enmity, Venus- Neutral, Saturn- Enemy.

In this way, you can know whether the house Jupiter is placed in is inimical or not. Zaddy's chart doesn't fulfill the condition of Gajakesari yoga. Hence, he will not have the royal status.

Note: If Gajakesari yoga is happening both from the Moon and ascendant, it is a very strong yoga. Results will fructify when the mahadasha/antardasha of Jupiter, Moon, or dasha of the depositor of Jupiter is going on.

Vipareet rajyoga

If the lords of trik houses VI, VIII, or XII are positioned in any other two houses other than his own, it is called vipareet rajyoga. Kingly status after a lot of struggles or after the failure of enemies. This yoga also provides excellent achievements.

How this yoga works is by making a connection with all three houses. Say in Cosmic man's chart Mars is VIII lord but placed in VI house. Then Mars by lordship controlling VIII, by position influencing VI, and by the seventh aspect influencing the XII house. Hence, the truest vipareet rajyoga comes to pass.

In Zaddy's chart, Mars is XII lord and placed in VIII house, also Jupiter is VIII lord and present in VIII, but VI lord Venus is present in VII house and not making a connection with the other two lords, therefore partial vipareet rajyoga will come to pass.

Amala yoga

If there are only benefics in the X from the Moon or ascendant, then this yoga is present. The native will be honoured by the king(government), enjoy great pleasures of life, liked by friends, helpful to others, pious and virtuous, long-lasting fame till stars and the Moon exist.

Zaddy's chart doesn't have any benefic in X house, therefore this yoga is not present.

Dharmakarmadhipati yoga

'Dharma' (lord of IX house), 'Karma' (lord of X house), 'adhipati' means lordship. So, whenever there is a connection of IX and X lord by aspect or conjunction or exchange, this yoga will come to pass. In cosmic man's chart, this will be the Jupiter (IX lord) and Saturn (X lord) connection. This will make the native sincere, devoted, righteous, and fortunate as well. This yoga is applicable even for a different ascendant; whenever Saturn and Jupiter make a connection with each other by mutual aspect, exchange, or conjunction. This yoga confers authority and prominent leadership in the organisation.

Note: *When IX and X lord make such a connection for other ascendants, we call it rajyoga but don't use the term dharmakarmadhipati. Many yogas are only specific to certain ascendants and do not apply to others. Hence needs to be checked on case-by-case basis.*

Solar yogas

Solar yogas are yogas with respect to the Sun. If there is a planet other than the Moon in the second house from Sun then **vesi** yoga, if the twelfth from the Sun then **vosi** yoga, if second as well as the twelfth from Sun is present then **ubhayachara** yoga. The below will occur if the planet involved other than the Moon is a benefic else results will be opposite.

Vesi: One born will have a balanced outlook, happy with even little wealth, tall and indolent, truthful.

Vosi: One born in this yoga is skilful, charitable, endowed with fame, learned, and strong.

Ubhayachara: One born in this yoga will be a king or equal to a king and be happy.

Note: In Zaddy's chart, Sun is in VII house. Second from the Sun are Mars, Mercury, and Jupiter. Hence **Vesi** *yoga is present in his chart. Repeat this exercise in your chart.*

Lunar yogas

Lunar yogas are yogas with respect to the Moon. If there is a planet other than the Sun in the second house from the Moon then **sunaphaa** yoga, if twelfth from the Moon is present then **anaphaa** yoga, if present in both the second as well as twelfth from the Moon then **duradhara** yoga is present.

Sunaphaa: One born with this yoga becomes a king or equal to a king, endowed with intelligence, wealth, fame, and self-earned wealth.

Sourabh Roy

Anaphaa: One born with this yoga becomes a king, free from diseases, virtuous, famous, charming, and happy.

Duradhara: Enjoys many pleasures, charitable. He owns vehicles and has excellent servants.

Note: In Zaddy's chart second and twelfth from the Moon do not have any planets(Rahu and Ketu are exceptions). Hence, the yoga is not present in his chart. Since sunaphaa yoga also talks of self-earned wealth it gives a clue that the native has the promise of an independent profession or business in his chart.

Chapter 10

Planetary period or dasha

Dashas are planetary time periods, classics mention a lot of dasha such as Vimshottari, Kalachakra, Chara, Yogini, etc. However, out of these the most used is the Vimshottari dasha system. We will look into vimshottari dasha only. It is based on janma nakshatra or the nakshatras the planet Moon is placed in the natal chart.

Nakshatras

Nakshatra are the lunar mansions used in Vedic astrology. It is the elliptical path ('Naks' -sky, 'Shetra' - area/map) of the moon through the stars. The moon cycle is of 27.3 days; the time it takes to travel through its orbit. Considering equal divisions of 27 lunar mansions of the 360º zodiac, each nakshatra spans out over 13.33º which are further divided into four padas (legs signified as Dharma, Artha, Kama and Moksha).

The 27 Nakshatras (lunar constellation) are; Ashwini, Bharani, Krittika, Rohini, Mrigasira, Ardra, Punarvasu, Pushya,

Ashlesha, Magha, Purva Phalguni, Uttara Phalguni, Hasta, Chitra, Swati, Vishakha, Anuradha, Jyestha, Mula, Purva Asadha, Uttara Asadha, Shravana, Dhanistha, Satabhishaj, Purva Bhadrapada, Uttara Bhadrapada, Revati.

As per the classic, the lifespan of humans in Kali Yuga will be 120 years. So the entire Vimshottari dasha equals 120 years where different planets are assigned different weights. The period of dasha for Sun is six years, Mars is seven, Moon is ten, Rahu is eighteen, Jupiter is sixteen, Saturn is nineteen, Mercury is seventeen, Ketu is seven, and Venus is twenty years respectively. It is calculated from Krittika nakshatra and follows the sequence of Sun, Moon, Mars, Rahu, Jupiter, Saturn, Mercury, Ketu, and Venus in that order respectively. Since there are 27 nakshatras therefore each planet will get the dasha lord of three nakshatras.

Nakshatras	Planet	Dasha duration
Krittika, Uttara Phalguni, Uttar Asadha	Sun	6

Nakshatras	Planet	Dasha duration
Rohini, Hasta, Shravana	Moon	10
Mrigasira, Chitra, Dhanistha	Mars	7
Ardra, Swati, Satabhishaj	Rahu	18
Punarvasu, Vishakha, Purva Bhadrapada	Jupiter	16
Pushya, Anuradha, Uttara Bhadrapada	Saturn	19
Ashlesha, Jyestha, Revati	Mercury	17
Magha, Moola, Ashwini	Ketu	7
Purva Phalguni, Poorva Asadha, Bharani	Venus	20

The above planets are the dasha lords of the respective nakshatras and not be confused as lords of nakshatras. The lord of these nakshatras are different deities. For example, Shravana's lordship is Vishnu. Dhanistha's lordship is Vasu.

Note: *Deities always supersede planets, and planets supersede ganas (Raksha, Manushya, Deva).*

Now recollect Zaddy's chart, his Moon is placed in Taurus at 10°, Rohini nakshatra falls in Taurus within the span of 10° - 23°20′ of Taurus. Therefore his janma nakshatra will become Rohini and the dasha lord becomes Moon. So his vimshottari dasha will start from the Moon and subsequently follow the above planetary order of dasha lordship i.e., after Moon, there will be dasha of Mars, Rahu, Jupiter, Saturn, Mercury, Ketu, Venus, and Sun respectively. These are called mahadasha. Now, mahadasha will have subsequent dasha such as antardasha which is a sub dasha. It is like breaking down the entire mahadasha into small modules and these modules again follow the same sequence as the mahadasha. In other words, if mahadasha is of the

Moon then within the sub dasha(antardasha), the sequence will be Moon, Mars, Rahu, Jupiter, Saturn, Mercury, Ketu, Venus, and Sun respectively. So Moon mahadasha is ten years and this ten years is further divided into nine proportionate periods starting from the Moon till Sun.

The computation of Vimshottari dasha will require a lot of calculations, therefore it is beyond the scope of the book. Moreover, the astrological software will compute the vimshottari dasha for you.

Vimshottari dasha accuracy becomes excellent only when the birth time is accurate. The more accurate the birth time, the closer the results. However, it is not possible for every native or even for a seasoned astrologer to rectify the birth chart accurately, either because the astrologer lacks skill or there is an uneasiness with clients to share their life events with a stranger. Due to this reason, a lot of different dasha came into existence and became popular as well. A few notable works involve the use of Kalachakra dasha as well as Char dasha. Since the purpose of this book is to make use of Jyotisha for yourself, the focus will be only on vimshottari dasha and it will be more than enough for you.

The mahadasha period will set the theme for the entire period, the antardasha period will bring the events and planetary transit will ensure either fulfilment or failure of such events.

For a promise to fulfill; mahadasha, antardasha, and planetary transit all three must align. The planet which is the mahadasha lord, the respective house owned by it, and the position it is in, will be the prime theme throughout the dasha.

So, when Zaddy was born his mahadasha lord was Moon, moon owns the III house in his chart (Taurus ascendant) and Moon occupies I house and aspect VII, therefore throughout the mahadasha of Moon I, III & VII remains prime. Antardasha lord planet will support by its position and aspect. Say, Zaddy is running the mahadasha of Moon and antardasha of Venus, then Venus is positioned in VII house and aspecting I house. So during that period, his I, III, and VII are of importance, so a possibility arises that Zaddy meets his first baby love, the day that event will happen will be determined by the transit of Venus for that year.

When multiple planets are present in one house, say Zaddy runs the dasha of Jupiter. His Jupiter owns the VIII and XI house. Also, the VIII house is a trik house plus it has three planets: Mercury, Mars, and Jupiter. So, the possibility of the VIII house will occur frequently during planetary transit. Hence, it would be extremely challenging for him to keep up with.

Summary of using Vimshottari dasha

A) Mahadasha lord makes the house owned by it, and its position and aspect active.

B) Antardasha lord makes the position and aspect active.

C) Planetary transit of antardasha/pratyantar dasha lord brings the possibilities.

D) Fast-moving planets such as the Moon, Mercury, Venus, and Sun will bring frequent windows for fulfilment of promises present in the D1 chart. Slow-moving planets such as Jupiter, Rahu and Saturn will bring a small window for the fulfilment of promise during the said dasha.

Chapter 11

Mundane astrology

Most asked questions of astrology as an opinion of the public data are:

Family, Self, Career prospect, Marriage or relationships, Progeny, Wealth, Luck or fortune, and health issues.

We already know the respective houses in the birth chart for the aforementioned queries. The planets owning those houses and their position will tell us the answer. Before you begin to answer any of them, you have to verify your birth time and then proceed. Keep a record of your analysis for future use else you have to repeat the entire process at a later stage. Always keep a diary or a journal once you start your journey with Jyotisha. It becomes a must. A few events may not seem interesting in the beginning but as you grow in this journey, mapping events with hora astrology (a sub-branch of astrology for help with queries that come to your mind at that point in time or blank chart prediction for an unknown person of interest) will become stronger.

We will look at example charts for different queries, how it works, and how to do it. We will club all queries into four segment

Dharma - career, life path, etc.
Artha- livelihood, profession, wealth, source of income, etc.
Kama- status, power, marriage, relationship, miscellaneous desire, etc.
Moksha - religion, pilgrimage, spiritual journey, occult, etc.

Sourabh Roy

Life path/Dharma

It is always decided by the day lord that one has to follow throughout his life. When a profession becomes aligned with one's dharma, grace follows as the native is playing his role in cosmic cosplay (refer to the book Cosmic Cosplay And The Naughty Beggar). If the profession and dharma are separate then the native has to struggle a lot and his efforts will go to waste. Consider a monkey who is looking at the sky and trying to fly like a bird, each day he jumps from a tree and falls, he put in years and years of effort, twenty hours a day of work and no result, and ended up blaming everything, whereas all he had to do was stay true his dharma; poking some humans, stealing lion cubs, stealing some food, wasting some fruits and destroying trees, becoming fodder for predators. Similarly, when we choose a profession or livelihood not based on who we are deep within, we jump into a race that has no winner. Most of the time it is also possible that due to lack of resources and support talent gets wasted but, if you keep the flame burning within even during frosty winds of life, a day will arrive when that spark ignites the ember of your success, or whatever the definition of success is for you.

If your day lord is Mercury, whatever may be your profession is, the influence of Mercury will be more prominent, which means you can be working in the metal industry but end up being the great spokesperson with a gift of gab, or you make miniature(Mercury) metal works   that are very intricate. If your day lord is Jupiter, whatever may be your profession, you end up teaching, guiding, advising or influencing related to Jupiter will remain evident throughout your work. If your day lord is Mars, say one becomes an actor(which is the influence of Venus; as it is the entertainment industry) then you will get roles of action, sports, or anything that represents the influence of Mars. Now, what kind of influence of planets will happen is a vast arena of computations, the house the planet is positioned in, the nakshatra theme, and the overall chart will determine those dynamics.

Say, Mars is connected with IV house in the chart and his day lord is Mars, the native is extremely qualified and works in banking sector, then you will witness his domain will be handling real estate, because Mars is now bringing the flavour of IV house along with. If the zodiac sign where Mars is positioned is a movable sign, the person will have to visit the location of those properties in person. If it is in a fixed sign, he could be sitting in the loan department. If Moon is the day lord and Moon is positioned in the XI house for a native, then he will nurture his elder sibling and his social network. The native can nurture good or bad traits depending upon the overall chart.

Career

If a career is the same as lifepath, it is best. But let us assume it is not the case and both are different, in such a scenario the mahadasha of the teenage years of a native becomes very vital. Those years are the building blocks of the future. You can't teach new tricks to an old dog, so when it is a puppy it will learn faster and absorb more. If there is a promise in the D1 chart but the teenage mahadasha doesn't support those, the native will miss out on that opportunity. It is like there are excellent yogas to become a public servant but in the teenage years, secondary education is not that great. On top of it, the supporting dasha is arriving late in life and the minimum age criteria of the respective examination is over. In such a scenario, it is very vital to have a long-term vision of your dasha as well. If you are selecting a profession it can be tough for you unless you have a supporting dasha. Professions may change in major mahadasha but dharma will remain intact throughout.

Check your current mahadasha which you are running and your day lord, if you are running the mahadasha of your day lord then fated events will happen for you. If you are running a different dasha, whether that planet is making a connection with your X house or its lord, then the possibility of change arises. For life path, only D1 chart is sufficient but, for profession, there is another divisional chart known as D10 which needs to be looked at. You can obtain the D10 chart from the software itself. The zodiac sign where the planet owns the X house or is positioned in X house or aspecting the X house all needs to be looked at.

Now, recall Zaddy's chart, his Saturn is placed in the IV house aspecting the X house(seventh aspect) and Saturn is also the X tenth lord. The X house is empty and it is not receiving any other planetary aspect other than Saturn. So for career, we need to look at Saturn in D10 or Dasamsa chart. In his D10 chart, Saturn falls in the dasamsa of Sagittarius and Mercury is also in the dasamsa of Sagittarius. So, we come back again to the D1 chart and check the position of Mercury. Mercury is in the VIII house in conjunction with

Mars(his day lord) and Jupiter. So now for certain, we can say the planets influencing the career will be Saturn, Mercury, Mars, and Jupiter.

His teenage mahadasha till seventeen years were of moon and mars, therefore we can say that he got the opportunity of supporting dasha for his career as well as the lifepath. Also, we can say his work will be connected to VIII house themes because his day lord is also present in that house.

Example chart 1

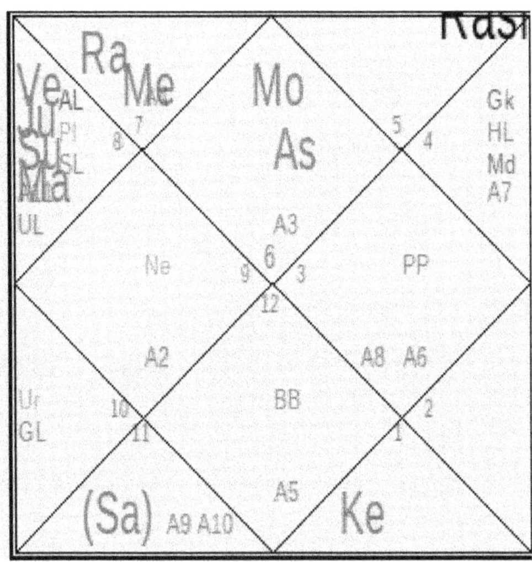

D1 chart.

Ascendant- 11o41', Sun - 2o16', Moon - 12o32', Mars- 27o25', Mercury - 29o47' , Jupiter- 25o58', Venus - 25o27', Saturn - 24o12', Rahu - 2o26' , Ketu - 2o26'. This snapshot is created in JHora software using Ayanamsa as 'Traditional Lahiri' and Nodes as 'True nodes'.

Sourabh Roy

Note: When using JHora software always make sure to set Ayanamsa as 'Traditional Lahiri' under the tab Preferences> Related to Calculations> Ayanamsa. And nodes as 'True position' under the tab Preferences> Related to Calculations > Planet calculation options.

In the above chart for career, the lord of X house is Mercury, and planetary aspects on X house is the eighth aspect of Mars. Mercury is positioned in II house with Rahu. II is of speech and vocals. Mars is in III house of skills, communication, etc. Now, the shastiamsa lordship(D60) of planets Sun, Moon, Mars, Mercury, Jupiter, Venus, Saturn, and Rahu are Atiseetala, Yama, Kinnara, Chandrarekha, Garala, Vahini, Chandramukhi, Yaksha. X lord Mercury is falling in dasamsa(D10) of Cancer and the Sun is also in dasamsa of Cancer. Native's day lord is Saturn. So we can say his life path and career are not making any connection, therefore they are incoherent. Hence, his career will be different and lifepath will be different. His four planets will determine the career Sun, Mercury, Mars, and Rahu.

Note: The day lord is always Vedic day i.e., the day starts and changes as per the rise of the Sun. So, if one is born at night, as per Julian's calendar his day will change after midnight but not his Vedic day.

Native teenage mahadasha is of Moon, Mars, and Rahu. Therefore the mahadasha is supporting career choices and planets. Now, we have to make the combination of shastiamsa lordship of the four planets Sun, Mars, Mercury, and Rahu. Sun is in atiseetala in III house of communication so the style of communication will be very soft and soothing. Mars is in Kinnara and we know Kinnara is in the court of Yaksha who are singers, dancers, poets, artists, etc. Yaksha also gives talents related to speech and Rahu is placed in II house in sign of Libra so here Rahu takes the shape of Venus. So we can say the profession of this person is connected to art, communication, oratory skills, speaking, signing, etc.

Native lifepath is connected to Saturn which rules V and VI in this chart and falls in shastiamsa of Chandramukhi. We know Chandramukhi is one of the aspects of the story of Ganga and V house is also children, so the most prominent story was of Devavrata aka Bhisma in the epic Mahabharata. For the native above, significance related to the V house becomes his life path.

Sourabh Roy

Exercise: *Repeat the above exercise with your chart and note your findings.*

Note: *Shastiamsa of the boss, rulers, governments, or any person with discretionary power are Kubera, Yama, Heramba, Bramha, Vishnu, Maheswara, Dandayudha, Indu, Sudha, Gulika, Khiteesa, Apampathi rest all other shastiamsa serves the above. This method is useful in finding the career. Say, X house or X lord is making a connection with yaksha, day lord is Saturday then one can say the person will be associated with the government or a public servant. Therefore, he has more possibility of clearing the requisite examinations if the dasha are supporting. Also, if ghora, marut, or karaladamshtra are associated with X house or lord and day lord is Mars, we can the native can be a sportsperson. If X house or X lord is connected with Vahini, dandayudha, and the day lord is Venus, then possibility of a paints and pigment business. If X house or X lord is connected with kaala, rakshasa, amrita, and the day lord is Venus, the native could be in sex work. If the native wants to do independent business or a contractor then his X lord must make a connection with a shastiamsa of discretionary power. If none is present in the chart, then choose service.*

Example chart 2

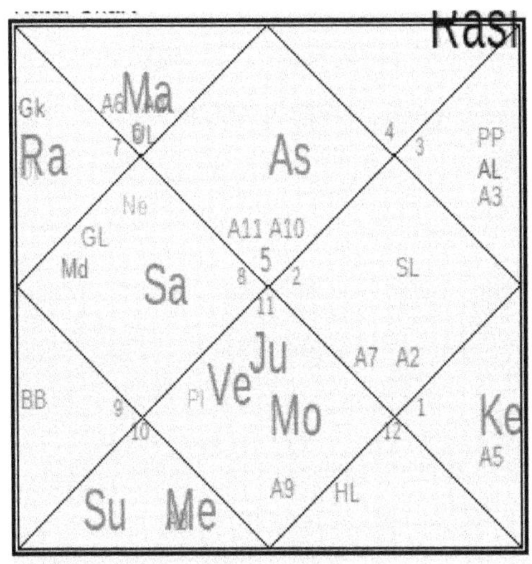

D1 chart

19 Jan 1809, 22:00 hrs, latitude 42N21, longitude 71W03, UTC -4, Vedic day - Thursday, Yoga- parigraha, karana - bava.

The day lord for the native is Jupiter. Therefore life path is connected to Jupiter. Jupiter owns the V and VIII houses in his chart. Jupiter is present with Moon and Venus in the VII house. Now, the shastiamsa lordship for each planet starting from Sun to Rahu is Kaala, Bhramana, Yaksha, Utpata, Dandayudha, Amrita, Vishadagdha, and Yama respectively.

His Moon is in VII house in the sign of Aquarius and in Bhramana shastiamsa, therefore the native has a wandering mind. Since the lord of VII house is Saturn (Vishadagdha), it is damaged by grief or depression. So wandering of mind due to depression. Also, his ascendant lord Sun is in VI house of debts and enemies along with II & XI house lord Mercury. Now, both are conjunct in Capricorn, again lord is Saturn is in malefic shastiamsa. Therefore the VI house is also damaged. Now, the Sun falls in Kaala and Mercury in Utpata shastiamsa both malefic, therefore damage to wealth, earning as well as body. Rahu is in III house and Ketu in IX house falls in Yama shastiamsa, again an extremely malefic shastiamsa. Rahu is in the sign of Libra, whose lord is Venus. So, here Rahu shape-shift into Venus and aspects IX house. Saturn is positioned in IV house in the sign of Mars, which is falling in Yaksha shastiamsa, a beneficial shastiamsa but Saturn is inimical to Mars and also to the ascendant lord Sun in this chart. So here Saturn will damage the IV house as well. Saturn's third aspect is on Sun and Mercury on VI house, Saturn's III aspect is always destructive, destroying the finances and earnings of the native; extreme poverty. Saturn's tenth aspect is on the ascendant, which gives his more effort to gain results. His IV and IX lord Mars is present in II house in an inimical sign Virgo. But, Mars is in beneficial shastiamsa so some defects will be neutralised. Mars is aspecting the V, VIII, and IX house with fourth, seventh, and eighth aspects respectively. Jupiter being lord of V and VIII is sitting in VII and aspecting the XI, I, and III by fifth, seventh, and ninth aspect respectively.

Now, look at how unfortunate the chart is, native's teenage mahadasha were Jupiter(2 years) and then Saturn. The mahadasha of the life path and his dharma; Jupiter was already finished before he began this journey. At two years he was running mahadasha of Jupiter and antardasha of Rahu, the native lost his father. At the age of , his Saturn mahadasha began, and he lost his mother. One sister died(III house; yama shastiamsa) and the elder brother drank himself to death. Adopted by another person, he got gambling and debts; II, XI lord damaged as well as VI house damaged. A teenage filled with penury. He served in the army for a few years(kaala, utpata), under an alias and started writing and publishing his poetry and other works. His poetry and literature were horror, thriller, or gore with a touch of romanticism. Rahu in yama shastiamsa in III house behaving as the poet Venus. Venus is also the lord of X house which is directly aspected by Saturn. Saturn is in vishadagdha shastiamsa gave him the melancholy and macabre theme in this work. Jupiter ninth aspect on III house gave him the quality of a critic. Jupiter in dandayudha shastiamsa(an aspect of sage Durvasa). Jupiter direct aspect on his ascendant gave him an irascible temper due to dandayudha shastiamsa. In the D10 chart, his X lord Venus falls in Leo navamsa, and Saturn and Jupiter fall in Libra navamsa, therefore his work involved themes of planet Sun, Venus, Saturn, and Jupiter. In the D9 chart, his XI(Mercury) and V(Jupiter) lord makes a connection, and he married his younger cousin who was only thirteen years old when he was twenty-seven, and later she died due to tuberculosis. His literary works were recognised as he was one of the first American writers in that particular genre of macabre and gothic romanticism.

'What is life without a little bit of pain, ain't that right my friend.' - Venus, Purva Bhadrapada, III house, Yama shastiamsa.

Sourabh Roy

Example chart 3

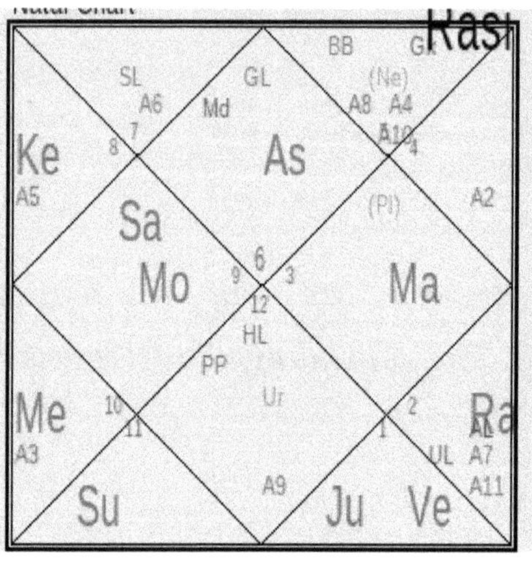

D1 Chart

5 March 1929, 19:15:30, latitude 75E08, longitude 14 N 46, UTC +5.30, Vedic day - Mars, karana -Vanija, Yoga- Vyati-pata.

The above chart is of a female native from an affluent family who ran away from her home at the age of 16 with her supposed husband to chase her dream of becoming an actress. Her husband betrayed and sold her into prostitution.

From there she rose to the ranks of a Madame, later a social activist for the rights of sex workers.

Day lord is Mars, therefore the life path will revolve around the themes of Mars. Mars is the lord of the III and VIII houses. Moon is positioned in the IV house with Saturn and receives planetary aspects from Mars (seventh aspect) and Jupiter (ninth aspect). Lagna lord Mercury is placed in the V house in the sign of Capricorn, which is friendly to Mercury. However, the eighth aspect of Mars is on Mercury. When the ascendant lord makes a connection with V or IX house and is well placed, the native is born with fortunes. Hence, she was born into an affluent family. The Shastiamsa lordships are Kaala, Kamalakara, Maya, Purishaka, Gulika, Maya, Marut, and Payodhi from Sun to Rahu, respectively. During the mahadasha of Venus and the antardasha of Mercury, she left her home. Venus is the lord of II and IX house and sits in the VIII house along with Jupiter. Jupiter is aspecting XII, II, and IV house. Jupiter is also the lord of the IV and VII houses. Mercury is the lord of X and Lagna. Mars is in Mrigasira nakshatra and Maya shastiamsa, it gave the search like the golden deer but here in this case it was the spotlight, the dream of an actress. Moon in Kamalakara gave her beautiful looks despite being conjunct with Saturn. Sun is placed in Kaala shastiamsa. Whenever the Sun, Moon, or lagna lord falls in Kaala shastiamsa, the seed is damaged. Moreover, it gives the native narcissistic tendencies. Since she didn't focus much on her education, it became easy for her to get duped and become a victim, Maya shastiamsa gave her the illusion that she had it all that takes to be an actress and nothing else was required, therefore she took the dire step as a teenager to leave home. Rahu in her ninth house in the sign of Taurus. Here, Rahu assumes the form of Venus in his mooltrikona rashi. Also, we know gulika is one of the shastiamsa that gives discretionary power; it is quite common for judges and solicitors. Here, it is giving native the power to command over other sex workers as a madame. Now, check her D10 chart. The lords and planets influencing the X house are Mars, Saturn, Moon, Mercury, and Venus. During her Moon mahadasha, she became like a mother to other sex workers as well as counselled younger girls to send them back home.

Now, the question that should come to your mind is, if everything is pre-determined why bother about free will? And that is where you need to reassess the chart if the placements are still the same. And her life-path had to be of Mars, she could have chosen luxury real estate business or insurance. Then also the themes would have been satisfied. VIII house denotes many things such as inheritance and insurance. Mars in Maya and aspect on IV house would have been the search for luxury real estate apartments. But all that would have required her to have an education. And this is where Jyotisha helps one person. If the information had been known to her at a young age she would have made her choices differently.

Note: Saturn and Mars mutually aspecting each other or in conjunction is always tough placement for a female native, if the shastiamsa lordships are malefic then even more brutal.

Sourabh Roy

"When wings are of air and passion is of the eternal flame, no one can douse such flame." - Saturn, Uttara Asadha, IX house, Dandayudha, and Davagani shastiamsa.

Key points

A) When life path and career become the same, you are in sync with the cosmic cosplay. Vedic day lord determines your fate and it can't be changed, rest you have free will. Few combinations of day lord with career.

For public servants; yaksha or kinnara, as both are serving in the courts of Kubera. Therefore, if you are aspiring for any public service examination or working with the government as a bureaucrat, it is necessary to have a connection with the above lordship.

For independent businesses, artists or industrialists any shastiamsa lordship that has discretionary power must be making a connection with the tenth lord or seventh lord, few are kshiteesa, dandayudha, gulika, yama, heramba, vishnu, brahma etc.

For adult industry or entertainment; Kaala, Raksha, Kroora, Ghora, Yama etc will make a connection with tenth lord or tenth house.

For musical skills; Saumya, Deva, Mridu, Amrita, Seetala or Atiseetala will make a connection with the second house as well as the tenth house. Also Vedic day lord connects with them.

For healing; Vishnu shastiamsa will make a connection, for heroes; Heramba, for educators, scholars or scientists; Brahma shastiamsa.

For sports, athletes, extremely dangerous sports; ghora shastiamsa will make a connection along with any Agni (davagani, vahini or kalapavaka).

For politicians; Bhramana as well as Praveena must make a connection.

For con-artist; Praveena and Vamsakshaya.

For astrologers; either of them must be there; Heramba, Vishnu, Brahma, Praveena.

For psychology; Praveena as well as Yama shastiamsa must be there.

For occult, mysticism, spirituality, or esoteric arts; Yama shastiamsa must be there.

For work in the guns and arsenal industry utpata must make a connection.

For agriculture, cosmetics, pottery, or sculpting purishaka shastiamsa must make a connection.

B) Always look for I, V, and IX house shastiamsa lordship, even if anyone is present (Brahma, Vishnu, Maheswara, Heramba, Kubera, Indu, Chandramukhi) there is blessing due to merit of immediate past birth.

C) Always compute all the possibilities of planets and their lordships also check D10 before arriving at any conclusion.

D)When you walk your life path, grace automatically follows irrespective of your status. You can be a barber or a tailor and could be an impeccable artist.

Chapter 12

Artha/Wealth

Different planet bestows different wealth. The more the strength of the planet, the stronger the results.

Sun	Status
Moon	Nourishment
Mars	Courage
Mercury	Intelligence
Jupiter	Wisdom
Venus	Pleasures
Saturn	Longevity
Rahu	Visionary
Ketu	Enlightenment

One native can't have the blessings of all planets no matter how fortunate the chart is. Examples of such are witnessed in the story of Ramayana, where Ravana; a scholar of Jyotisha, planned the conception to bring forth his son Meghnad, who later conquered Indra but died young because Saturn was the only planet that refused to fall in line. It is a lesson, a reminder for all of us.

Now, coming to the bhavas in the natal chart.

XI house is the house of gains from your career. II house is accumulated wealth or savings. So, when you save your earnings, that is seen through II house. Your expenses are XII house. Recall Zaddy's chart, his II house lord is Mercury and XI lord is Jupiter, both placed in the VIII house. So his earnings and wealth will come from VIII house related work, inheritance, sudden gains, gains due to failure of enemies (vipareet rajayoga), etc.

Take the chart in example 1:

II lord is Venus, XI lord is Moon and their respective depositor are Mars, and Mercury respectively. Rahu and Mercury is in II. Also XII house of expenses and its lord Sun is with Mars, Venus. Therefore gains will be from Mercury and Moon and their respective significance.

Rahu and Mercury if behaving beneficial for the native then investments such as crypto, equity, gambling, betting, etc.

Sun - government bonds, sovereign schemes, etc.

Saturn - metals or anything long-term.

Mars - real estate.

Venus - luxury goods, art, females, silver.

Moon - food industry, mother.

Jupiter - gold.

Ketu- sudden gains that are owed to you.

Exercise: Repeat the above exercise with your chart and note your findings.

Chapter 13

Kama/Desire

The position of the Moon tells us the desire, and the opposite house is the means to achieve it. We have already gone through it in chapter 4. In Zaddy's chart, Moon is in the I house so he wants attention to himself, and expects it from the VII house.

Marriage or relationship

The VII house is connected with marriage. V house is connected with the desire of your partner (V house is eleventh from VII house; a concept of bhavat bhavam) and the XI house is connected to the fulfilment of the native's desire. So whenever there is a connection between the seventh lord and eleventh lord or the houses involved either by aspect or conjunction, or either of them falling in another navamsa, the possibility of love marriage occurs. Recall Zaddy's chart, his VII lord is Mars, XI lord is Jupiter and V lord is Mercury, all conjunct in VIII house, but Mars is in Libra navamsa, Mercury and Jupiter is in Cancer navamsa. Mars is also the XII house. So the possibility is present in the D1 chart but incoherent in D9. Moreover, whenever marriage or kids happen, there will be a sudden or unexpected event in the family and it could be a bittersweet moment. If the entire promise is nullified in the D60 chart, then it will not fructify. A female native will behave as her Venus placement and a male native will behave as his Mars placement when they are single. But, in a relationship, the placement of Venus will become prime for male natives and Mars for female natives, respectively. If each other's Mars and Venus are in similar elements (air, earth, water, fire, ether), then the chemistry is strong.

In example 1, VII lord Jupiter is aspecting the XI house as well as VII house, XI lord is Moon aspecting the VII house, V lord Saturn is aspecting Jupiter by tenth aspect. Also, Saturn is in the navamsa of Venus, Jupiter, and Venus is in the navamsa of Saturn, and Moon is in the navamsa of Mars. Therefore, here also the connection of VII and V lord is strong in D1 as well as coherent in Navamsa. Therefore, the possibility becomes more strong in the chart. But again, the final say will always be D60 chart. In some cases where marriage is said to be out of love is a marriage of convenience unless V, or XI or both are involved.

Note: *Bhavat bhavam means to count the same number of houses from a house which is mirroring the significance of your chart. If the III house is your brother and you need to know about the influence of your brother's wife from your natal chart, then the seventh from the III house is the IX house. Hence, IX house will reflect the wife of your brother. Bhavat bhavam should only be applied when we want to know about other family members and their influence on us. Bhavat bhavam can't replace the unique natal chart of the person concerned.*

Sexual compatibility

Sexual compatibility is determined by the respective planet. In addition to it, the eighth house shows your sexual organs. Therefore VIII lord, VIII house, and the planetary aspects it is receiving, all together determine the strength and the type of the sexual organ. Emotional compatibility is known through birth(janma) nakshatra. If both emotional and physical compatibility are coherent, the couple has a strong bond. If it is incoherent then the bond is weak. Few shastiamsa lordships will give controlled sexuality, few will give normal, and few will give loose morals. The complete chart will decide whether the native will act upon it or not. Although every person comes from a different ethnicity or lineage, therefore the genes will come into play for their physical appearance. However, if the ethnicity, lineage or religion, etc factors are considered constant; sexual organs are broadly classified into six animals.

For males: Rabbit, Bull, Horse.
For females: Doe, Mare, Elephant.

Ideal connection:
Rabbit- Doe,(Mars, Mercury)
Bull- Mare,(Sun, Venus)
Horse-Elephant,(Saturn, Jupiter)

If the VIII lord falls in a shastiamsa which is malefic and there is no planetary aspect on the VIII house or VIII lord then there will be a defect of the sexual organ. Say, VIII lord falls in atiseetala and the native is a male, then it could give erectile dysfunction and, if the native is female she has least interest or satisfaction through intercourse. In such a scenario, if the other partner's chart is making an aspect to the VIII house plus has a presence of Agni(Vahini, Davagani, Kalapavaka) the defect can be alleviated.

When two people come into a union, their composite chart also comes into the union, one affects the other. The person with the stronger planet will influence the other person's respective house and vice-versa. The couple will have changes in their physical appearance, emotional state, or even their destiny i.e., alone they will behave differently than in a relationship with a particular person as the charts will be influencing one another.

Chapter 14

Moksha/Liberation

Moksha or liberation is getting closer to the truth, either it is your version of truth or the absolute truth. In search for either of them, one has to acknowledge the creator, the supreme consciousness itself. You may not believe in it but it believes in you. The whole crux of Gita as narrated by Sri Krishna was to seek him, know about him, and worship him in the form of dharma and karma that one is meant to do. If as a seeker your pursuit has ended then, what lord Krishna says is 'Come back to my play and dance again' which may seem interesting at first but once you understand the futility of the Maya, you will lose the desire to come back and participate. And that is exactly what Sri Krishna wants you to do. Live like a yogi(follow your dharma) and if life is presenting you with bhoga (indulgences), enjoy like a bhogi but don't get attached to it, know everything is temporary only karma is permanent.

As for spiritual pursuit, the chart D20 or bisamsa should be looked into.

Past life in a chart

Only two people can know about their past lives, one is yourself and another one is a yogi, other than that it is not feasible to know it. Any such tall claims from anyone else are illusionary or fraudulent.

Saturn's aspect on the Moon makes one pessimist, Jupiter's aspect on the Moon makes one optimistic, and Saturn and Jupiter both aspecting or conjunct with the Moon make one realist. In the birth chart, the Moon is memory and the reason for birth, Jupiter is wisdom, and Saturn is longevity. So when the Moon receives the aspect of both Saturn and Jupiter or in conjunction with either planet and aspect from the other. It will give rise to the possibility of knowing one's past life. But, just having the placement will not ensure it but the native has to be a seeker. Another placement is Ketu in the I house of the natal chart. This also gives the possibility of remembering past lives but here the condition of being a seeker is a must. An astrologer can't tell you about your past life unless he is a yogi himself.

A yogi will not practice astrology as a profession let alone commercially. One must proceed with caution in fantasy tales.

Sourabh Roy

Miscellaneous

Vastu/Architecture

Vastu is an integral part of India when constructing homes, temples, or any building or purchasing any property. Vastu will be based on the owner of that property. If the owner's Mars is afflicted or IV lord is afflicted then the house will have vastu problems. Also, if there are many members in a family, it is quite possible that for a few members that house may not be fortunate as per their natal chart. In such a scenario, one has to leave his home and find settlement in a foreign country or away from his native place. Vastu shastra in itself is an entire subject of study and beyond the scope of this book. However, there are a few key points from the perspective of Jyotisha that one must keep in mind. We have already acquainted ourselves with different direction and their corresponding planetary lords in the initial chapters. Apart from that, each direction has a deity associated with it, East - Indra, West - Varuna, North - Kubera, South- Yama, North East- Ishan, North West- Vayu, South East- Agni, South West - Nirruti. So, next time wherever you stay, whether it is travel for business or leisure, mark the directions in those places and observe the surroundings in that area and note it down. For example, if you see a coffee shop in a certain direction, note it with direction. Repeat this exercise at your residence as well, you will surprised to witness the theme of your birth chart playing out similarly as it happened at your residential place. It is an exercise to complete if you are interested in Vastu else optional.

Initiation of mundane task

Performing tasks related to specific days is always beneficial in the natural state.

Beginning of new ventures on Sunday, Thursday, and Wednesday.

Entertainment work, beauty, and arts on Fridays.

Ritual, worship, or special occasion on Monday, or Thursday.

Travel activities on Tuesday.

Work related to de-cluttering should be done on Saturday.

If Rahu and Mercury are strong in your chart prefer online mode else prefer brick-and-mortar stores or in-person.

Sourabh Roy

Note: if the said planet is malefic for the native the balance should be observed as the per law of balance or law of number 3(refer to the book Laws of Karma through the eyes of a child). If Mars is malefic for the native perform that work on Wednesday. For extremely specific occasions such as marriage, one needs to look at panchang and other details which is beyond the scope of the book.

Do's and Don'ts

A) Always verify birth time to the nearest possible seconds because D60 will vary even for twins. Complete this exercise before predicting or identifying themes in your birth chart.

B) Don't compare your life path or chart with another person even though the date of birth, place, or time is close. The reason is D60 ascendant varies within five seconds. Each person is unique in his own way. So the experience may be similar for two people, but how they perceive, understand, and act will be vastly different.

C) Always mind your own chart. Don't try to read another person's chart, or comment unless you are ready to take accountability for your choice of words. Moreover, in Jyotisha spoken words have consequences as it deals the with occult; which means Yama.

D) Don't put your birth chart on a website or any application that collects, saves and abuses your data. It is your blueprint and only you have your best interest.

E) Always note the birth time for a newborn the moment the child breathes and cries. Time of birth in your birth certificate will most likely be incorrect, at least by five to fifteen minutes. Don't try to force conception or delivery as per panchang or date, birth and death are pre-ordained. The soul has chosen the womb.

F) Any public birth data available for any celebrity has 98% probability of incorrect birth time. One should not gauge his prowess on celebrity charts. The more diverse charts across the horizon you can look at, the better the understanding.

G) A chart is either fortunate or unfortunate, it is based on the accumulation of merits and demerits respectively. Each chart will have both in some proportion. When the proportion is at an end. It behaves like Yin-Yang. But for the major population, it will be in between. One should not be proud or dissatisfied with one's chart. If your chart is good, you are already a champion therefore your focus is to retain that title for your next lineage by checking your dharma and karma. If your chart is unfortunate then your focus should not be on Jyotisha but completely on karma, the merits will fructify in your children and lineage.

H) Do not search for predicting death or such events. In each month, there are always two days when the possibility of a person leaving this world can happen. But the actual event only happens when planetary dasha, transit, planet, and hora all come together, it is only on that day such an event occurs. Other than "akal mrityu" or sudden deaths, most of the time natives will know that his or her time has arrived, but others may not know of it.

I) Don't mock an unfortunate chart or native with one, you will add some of his karma to your plate. Punya(virtue) and papa(sin) of parents are passed on to children, one must always be wary of that. It comes late but it always comes.

J) Whenever a planet is said to be beneficial or malefic, it is with respect to its natural traits. It has nothing to do with the native. A benefic planet can destroy a native and a malefic planet can become a boon as well.

K) The priority of understanding themes in a natal chart will always be day lord > zodiac sign > houses and their respective shastiamsa > nakshatras > planets and conjunctions > planetary aspects > planetary period or dasha > navamsa. Day lord is the day you were born, say one native is born on Tuesday therefore his day lord becomes Mars. Day lord denotes dharma and parabdha karma(fate). In addition to it, the shastiamsa in which Mars(in this case) falls in the D1 chart becomes an extremely important part of the native's fate.

L) All twelve houses in a chart are connected just like our entire body is an amalgamation of different limbs all working together. Any remedy done for any specific house will affect the other house as well. So, one must know the trade-off for any remedy if done at all. Say, if you choose Hades as your video game character then you can't have favour from Zeus and vice-versa. In Jyotisha also, propitiating one planet may disturb the other enemy planet.

M) There are different schools of thought in Jyotisha, be okay with "agree to disagree".

N) Everyone you meet is either a service provider or a client in the cosmic cosplay.

We have reached the end of the book, whatever you have learned so far, you need to apply all of it together in your chart. It will take time but eventually, you will get there. You will not be able to apply it to another person's chart because the skills required for that are advanced and not meant to be shared but rather earned. With best wishes, I leave you on this journey.